TRANSMATH™

Developing Number Sense

Interactive Text

John Woodward
Mary Stroh

Cambium
LEARNING®

BOSTON, MA | LONGMONT, CO

ISBN 13: 978-160697-043-0
ISBN: 1-60697-043-7

181981/2-11

Printed in the United States of America
Published and distributed by

Cambium
LEARNING®
Sopris West®

4093 Specialty Place • Longmont, CO 80504 • (303) 651-2829
www.sopriswest.com

TABLE OF CONTENTS

Name _____ Date _____

Skills Maintenance
Basic Addition Facts

Activity 1

Solve the problems using mental math.

1. $7 + 8$ _____

2. $9 + 2$ _____

3. $8 + 5$ _____

4. $7 + 4$ _____

5. $8 + 7$ _____

6. $9 + 9$ _____

7. $7 + 7$ _____

8. $2 + 8$ _____

9. $6 + 8$ _____

10. $6 + 9$ _____

11. $3 + 6$ _____

12. $4 + 1$ _____

13. $9 + 8$ _____

14. $5 + 9$ _____

15. $6 + 7$ _____

16. $6 + 5$ _____

17. $3 + 9$ _____

18. $9 + 7$ _____

19. $3 + 7$ _____

20. $8 + 8$ _____

21. $2 + 3$ _____

Name _____ Date _____

%÷ Apply Skills
Place Value in Whole Numbers

Activity 1

Write the numbers in the place value chart.

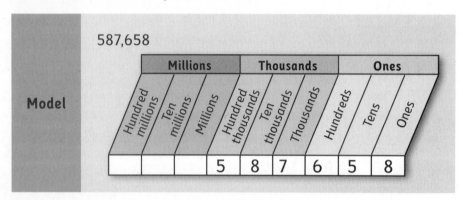

1. 6,421,359

Millions			Thousands			Ones		
Hundred millions	Ten millions	Millions	Hundred thousands	Ten thousands	Thousands	Hundreds	Tens	Ones

2. 500,407

Millions			Thousands			Ones		
Hundred millions	Ten millions	Millions	Hundred thousands	Ten thousands	Thousands	Hundreds	Tens	Ones

Name _____ Date _____

3. 21,058

Millions			Thousands			Ones		
Hundred millions	Ten millions	Millions	Hundred thousands	Ten thousands	Thousands	Hundreds	Tens	Ones

4. 105,009,670

Millions			Thousands			Ones		
Hundred millions	Ten millions	Millions	Hundred thousands	Ten thousands	Thousands	Hundreds	Tens	Ones

Activity 2

Write the values of the digits underlined.

Model	2_7_4,145	____70,000____

1. 348,_5_97 _____

2. _1_23,405 _____

3. 50_8_,112,485 _____

4. 3_0_0,001 _____

Name _____ Date _____

Problem-Solving Activity
Reading Word Problems Carefully

Read each problem carefully. Decide what the problem is asking.

Problem

There were 5,200 hot dogs sold at the ballpark last night. The attendance was 14,507. The hot dogs cost $3.75 each. The night before, there were 4,100 hot dogs sold. The attendance that night was 17,129. The owner of the ballpark wants to know how many hot dogs were sold at the last two games.

1. What is the problem asking for?

_____

_____

Problem

Sean met five friends at the arcade. He had $20 to spend. He spent $3 on air hockey. His friends each played six games. Sean spent $10 on video games. Then he spent $2 for a drink and a snack. He earned 175 tickets from the video games. His friend Kevin earned 200 tickets. Sean's mother asked him how much he spent at the arcade. What was his answer?

2. What is the problem asking for?

_____

_____

mBook **Reinforce Understanding**
Use the *mBook Study Guide*
to review lesson concepts.

Name _____ Date _____

 ## Skills Maintenance
Place Value

Activity 1

Answer the questions about place value for the number 896,403,157.

1. What is the value of the digit 6? _____

2. What digit is in the thousands place? _____

3. What is the value of the digit 5? _____

4. What digit is in the ten millions place? _____

5. What is the value of the digit 7? _____

6. What place is the zero in? _____

Name _____ Date _____

Apply Skills
Thinking About Numbers by Place Value

Activity 1

Solve the basic and extended facts.

1. $4 + 9$ _____ $40 + 90$ _____ $400 + 900$ _____

2. $7 + 8$ _____ $70 + 80$ _____ $700 + 800$ _____

3. $6 + 5$ _____ $60 + 50$ _____ $600 + 500$ _____

4. $7 + 9$ _____ $70 + 90$ _____ $700 + 900$ _____

Activity 2

Write the numbers in expanded form.

1. 543 _____

2. 1,005 _____

3. 605 _____

4. 2,012 _____

Name _____ Date _____

Activity 3

Write the numbers in standard form.

1. $900 + 70 + 2$ _____

2. $400 + 0 + 1$ _____

3. $5,000 + 0 + 70 + 2$ _____

4. $7,000 + 300 + 0 + 1$ _____

5. $8,000 + 0 + 10 + 3$ _____

Name _____ Date _____

Problem-Solving Activity
Reading Important Information

Read each problem carefully. Decide what the problem is asking. Write your answers on the lines provided. Then underline all the important information needed to solve the problem.

Problem

Nick has 25 CDs. They each cost about $15. His CD player cost $60. He likes only one song on each CD. He can download the songs he likes for about $5 each. How much money could Nick save if he downloads the songs he likes instead of buying CDs?

1. What is the problem asking for?

_____

_____

Problem

Jared likes to play arcade games at the mall. He collects tickets from playing the games, and he saves them. He is saving for a big prize that costs 7,500 tickets. He currently has 2,500 tickets. He spends about $10 and earns 500 tickets each time he visits the arcade. How many more trips to the arcade will it take before Jared has enough tickets to buy the big prize?

2. What is the problem asking for?

_____

_____

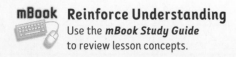

mBook **Reinforce Understanding**
Use the *mBook Study Guide*
to review lesson concepts.

Name _____ Date _____

 ## Skills Maintenance
Basic and Extended Addition Facts

Activity 1

Solve the basic and extended facts.

1. 9 + 8 _____   90 + 80 _____   900 + 800 _____

2. 6 + 7 _____   60 + 70 _____   600 + 700 _____

3. 9 + 4 _____   90 + 40 _____   900 + 400 _____

Expanded Form

Activity 2

Write the numbers in expanded form.

1. 407 _____

2. 312 _____

3. 650 _____

4. 9,096 _____

Name _____ Date _____

%÷ Apply Skills
Addition Problems in Expanded Form

Activity 1

Rewrite the problems in expanded form. Do not find the sums.

Model	24 + 83	20 | 4 + 80 | 3

1.   37
  + 42   + |

2.   29
  + 95   + |

Activity 2

Rewrite the problems in standard form. Do not find the sums.

Model	30 | 7 + 50 | 4	37 + 54

1.   60 \| 8
 + 40 \| 1   + _____

2.   60 \| 5
 + 80 \| 0   + _____

3.   30 \| 7
 + 80 \| 2   + _____

4.   300 \| 0 \| 7
 + 500 \| 0 \| 0   + _____

Problem-Solving Activity
Finding What the Problem is Asking For

Read each problem carefully. Decide what the problem is asking. Write your answers on the lines provided. Then underline all the important information needed to solve the problem.

Problem

The Blue Jays hit 24 home runs in June and 28 home runs in July. In August, the team's pitcher had two games with 15 strikeouts. In August, the Blue Jays hit 21 home runs. The coach wants to know how many home runs the Blue Jays hit in June and July together.

1. What is the problem asking for?

_____

_____

Problem

It takes five hours to fly from San Francisco to New York City. It takes another seven hours to fly from New York City to Rome. Many people travel this route. Andrea is traveling from San Francisco to New York to Rome. She wants to know how long the two flights are together.

2. What is the problem asking for?

_____

Problem

Leroy and Jamaal went to the movies on Saturday afternoon. Each ticket cost $6.50, and they bought snacks. Leroy bought popcorn and a drink for $5, and Jamaal just bought a drink for $2. When Leroy got home, his mom wanted to know how much he and Jamaal spent at the movies. Leroy's mom had just gotten home from work.

3. What is the problem asking for?

_____

mBook **Reinforce Understanding**
Use the *mBook Study Guide*
to review lesson concepts.

Name _____ Date _____

 Skills Maintenance
Basic and Extended Addition Facts

Activity 1

Solve the basic and extended facts.

1. 90 + 40 _____

2. 6 + 5 _____

3. 60 + 50 _____

4. 7 + 8 _____

5. 70 + 80 _____

6. 8 + 9 _____

7. 900 + 400 _____

8. 700 + 800 _____

9. 80 + 90 _____

10. 9 + 4 _____

11. 800 + 900 _____

12. 600 + 500 _____

Name _____ Date _____

%÷ Apply Skills
Expanded Addition

Activity 1

Add using expanded addition. Then write the sums in standard form.

Model	$\begin{array}{r} 24 \\ + 31 \\ \hline \end{array}$	$\begin{array}{r} 20\;\vert\;4 \\ +\;30\;\vert\;1 \\ \hline 50\;\vert\;5 \end{array}$	Answer _____55_____

1. $\begin{array}{r} 37 \\ + 42 \\ \hline \end{array}$ +   Answer _____

2. $\begin{array}{r} 61 \\ + 25 \\ \hline \end{array}$ +   Answer _____

3. $\begin{array}{r} 74 \\ + 13 \\ \hline \end{array}$ +   Answer _____

4. $\begin{array}{r} 68 \\ + 31 \\ \hline \end{array}$ +   Answer _____

Name _____ Date _____

✎ Problem-Solving Activity
Using Bar Graphs to Display Data

Use the bar graph to answer the questions.

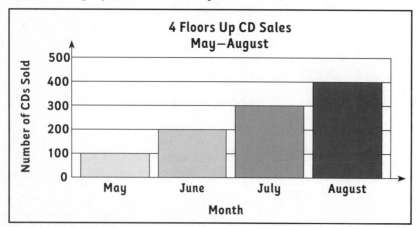

1. What is the title of the graph?

    _____

2. What is the label of the horizontal axis of the graph?

    _____

3. What is the label of the vertical axis of the graph?

    _____

4. What is the scale of the vertical axis?

    _____

5. What is the interval of the scale?

    _____

mBook **Reinforce Understanding**
Use the *mBook Study Guide*
to review lesson concepts.

Name _____ Date _____

 ## Skills Maintenance
Basic and Extended Addition Facts

Activity 1

Solve the basic and extended addition facts.

1. 4 + 9 _____

2. 9 + 4 _____

3. 60 + 50 _____

4. 50 + 60 _____

5. 80 + 90 _____

6. 90 + 80 _____

Expanded Addition

Activity 2

Add using expanded addition. Then write the sums in standard form.

1. 37
 + 51   + ____|____   Answer _____

2. 33
 + 46   + ____|____   Answer _____

Name _____ Date _____

 Problem-Solving Activity
Creating Bar Graphs

Create a bar graph that shows the CD sales for 4 Floors Up over the four-month period. Be sure to include a title for the graph, and label the horizontal axis and the vertical axis.

The data show how many CDs the band 4 Floors Up sold over a period of four months:

January: 200 CDs sold

February: 300 CDs sold

March: 500 CDs sold

April: 600 CDs sold

Title _____

mBook Reinforce Understanding
Use the *mBook Study Guide* to review lesson concepts.

Name _____ Date _____

 Skills Maintenance
Extended Addition Facts

Activity 1

Solve the extended facts.

1. 500 + 400 _____
2. 40 + 50 _____
3. 300 + 700 _____
4. 90 + 80 _____
5. 80 + 30 _____
6. 300 + 800 _____
7. 60 + 20 _____
8. 200 + 600 _____
9. 400 + 500 _____
10. 50 + 40 _____
11. 900 + 800 _____
12. 80 + 90 _____

Name _____ Date _____

 Apply Skills
More Expanded Addition

Activity 1

Add using expanded addition. Then write the sums in standard form.

1.   312
    + 457   +    Answer _____

2.   207
    + 691   +   Answer _____

3.   566
    + 303   +   Answer _____

4.   600
    + 399   +   Answer _____

Name _____   Date _____

Problem-Solving Activity

Analyzing Data in a Bar Graph

Use the bar graph to answer the questions.

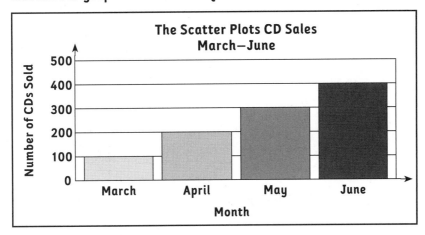

1. During which month were the most CDs sold?

   _____

2. During which month were the fewest CDs sold?

   _____

3a. What were the total CD sales during March and April?

   _____

3b. What extended fact did you use to find the answer?

   _____

4. If the Scatter Plots sell 600 CDs in July, what can you say about the trend?

   _____

mBook Reinforce Understanding
Use the *mBook Study Guide*
to review lesson concepts.

Name _____ Date _____

 Skills Maintenance
Basic Addition Facts

Activity 1

Complete the basic and extended facts.

1. 9 + _____ = 17   90 + _____ = 170   900 + _____ = 1,700

2. 8 + _____ = 17   80 + _____ = 170   800 + _____ = 1,700

3. _____ + 4 = 13   _____ + 40 = 130   _____ + 400 = 1,300

4. _____ + 9 = 13   _____ + 90 = 130   _____ + 900 = 1,300

Name _____ Date _____

 Apply Skills

Regrouping in Expanded Addition

Activity 1

Add using expanded addition. Then write the sums in standard form.

1.   57
   + 28   + ___|___   Answer _____

2.   45
   + 16   + ___|___   Answer _____

3.   46
   + 37   + ___|___   Answer _____

4.   271
   + 119   + ___|___|___

               + ___|___|___

               Answer _____

Name _____ Date _____

Problem-Solving Activity
Finding Information in Tables

Read each word problem carefully. Decide what the problem is asking for.

Hipster Records' CD Sales January–April	
Band	**CD Sales**
The Hammerheads	$30,000
4 Floors Up	$19,000
The Scatter Plots	$12,000
Three Ears	$6,000

Problem

Hipster Records is interested in how much more money the top-selling CD made from January to April than the next best-selling CD. The amounts listed in the chart show sales over four months. The amounts do not include sales after April.

1. What is the problem asking for?

    _____

    _____

Problem

The Hammerheads have become a very popular band. When their new CD came out, it was Hipster Records' best-selling CD. The new CD was called *On the Head*. From January to April, *On the Head* made $30,000. The Hammerheads' first CD was called *Claw Hammer*. It only made $5,000. Hipster Records wants to know how much more *On the Head* has made than *Claw Hammer*.

2. What is the problem asking for?

    _____

    _____

mBook **Reinforce Understanding**
Use the *mBook Study Guide*
to review lesson concepts.

Name _____ Date _____

 Skills Maintenance
Basic and Extended Addition Facts

Activity 1

Complete the basic and extended addition facts.

1. 2 + 9 = _____   90 + 20 = _____   200 + 900 = _____

2. 3 + 7 = _____   70 + 30 = _____   300 + 700 = _____

3. _____ + 8 = 13   _____ + 50 = 130   _____ + 800 = 1,300

4. _____ + 5 = 13   _____ + 50 = 130   _____ + 500 = 1,300

Name _____ Date _____

 Apply Skills
Comparing Methods of Regrouping

Activity 1

Add using expanded addition. Then write the sums in standard form.

1.   47
    + 35   + | Answer _____
                      |

2.   29
    + 18   + | Answer _____
                      |

Activity 2

Find the sums from Activity 1 using traditional addition.

1.   47   2.   29
    + 35   + 18

Activity 3

Compare traditional addition with expanded addition.
Which method do you like better? Why?

_____

_____

_____

_____

_____

Name _____ Date _____

Problem-Solving Activity
Creating a Graph From a Table of Data

Use the table to create a bar graph. Determine an appropriate scale for the data. Be sure to label the graph carefully.

The Hammerheads January–April CD Sales	
Month	**Number of CDs Sold**
January	250
February	500
March	750
April	1,000

Title _____

mBook Reinforce Understanding
Use the *mBook Study Guide* to review lesson concepts.

Name _____ Date _____

 Skills Maintenance
Basic and Extended Addition Facts

Activity 1

Complete the basic and extended facts.

1. 4 + 9 = _____

2. _____ = 40 + 90

3. 900 + 400 = _____

4. 6 + _____ = 13

5. 130 = _____ + 60

6. _____ + 600 = 1,300

7. _____ + 8 = 12

8. 120 = _____ + 80

9. 1,200 = 800 + _____

10. 9 + _____ = 14

11. 90 + _____ = 140

12. 1,400 = _____ + 900

Name _____ Date _____

 Apply Skills
More Methods of Regrouping

Activity 1

Add using expanded addition. Then write the sums in standard form.

1.   239
    + 25   + | | _____   Answer _____

2.   576
    + 47   + | | _____   Answer _____

Activity 2

Find the sums from Activity 1 using traditional addition.

1.   239   2.   576
    + 25   + 47

Name _____ Date _____

 Problem-Solving Activity
Posing Questions From a Graph

Try posing a question and answering it. The questions should be based on the observations given in the problem.

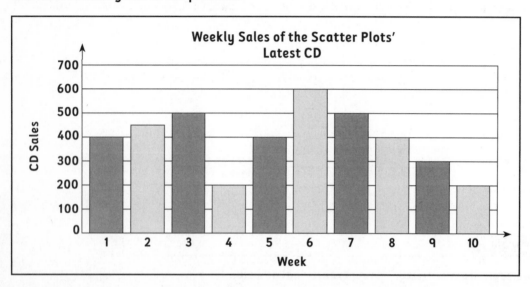

Finish each problem by writing a question. Then answer the question.

1. Cyndee has been looking over the graph. She notices that Week 6 was the best week for sales. She also notices that Week 4 was the worst week for sales.

   _____

   _____

2. Cyndee notices that there is a trend in sales over the last five weeks. For every week, sales are less than the week before. Hipster Records stops advertising for a CD when its sales drop below $200 a week.

   _____

   _____

   _____

mBook Reinforce Understanding
Use the *mBook Study Guide*
to review lesson concepts.

Name _____ Date _____

Skills Maintenance
Basic Addition Facts

Activity 1

Complete the basic facts.

1. $6 +$ _____ $= 12$
2. _____ $+ 6 = 13$
3. $4 + 8 =$ _____

4. _____ $= 8 + 4$
5. _____ $+ 7 = 14$
6. $13 =$ _____ $+ 6$

7. $12 =$ _____ $+ 8$
8. $4 +$ _____ $= 12$
9. $17 = 8 +$ _____

10. $9 +$ _____ $= 17$
11. $9 + 9 =$ _____
12. _____ $= 9 + 9$

Traditional Addition

Activity 2

Find the sums using traditional addition.

1. $\begin{array}{r} 38 \\ + 54 \\ \hline \end{array}$
2. $\begin{array}{r} 427 \\ + 92 \\ \hline \end{array}$
3. $\begin{array}{r} 306 \\ + 49 \\ \hline \end{array}$

Name _____ Date _____

%÷<x Apply Skills
Numbers on a Number Line

Activity 1

Estimate the numbers represented by the dots on the number lines.

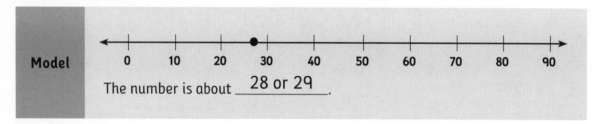

Model

The number is about ___28 or 29___.

1.

The number is about _____.

2.

The number is about _____.

3.

The number is about _____.

mBook **Reinforce Understanding**
Use the *mBook Study Guide*
to review lesson concepts.

30   Unit 1 • Lesson 10

Name _____ Date _____

Skills Maintenance
Extended Addition Facts

Activity 1

Complete the extended addition facts.

1. 700 + 900 = _____

2. 600 + _____ = 1,300

3. 70 + 50 = _____

4. 130 = 60 + _____

5. 50 + _____ = 130

6. _____ + 600 = 1,300

7. 1,300 = 500 + _____

8. 900 + 700 = _____

9. 1,200 = 500 + _____

Traditional Addition

Activity 2

Add using traditional addition.

1.   63
    + 42

2.   89
    + 12

3.   367
    + 428

Name _____ Date _____

%÷ Apply Skills
<=× Estimating Sums by Rounding

| Activity 1 |

Round the numbers to the greatest place value. Then estimate the sums. Check your estimates with a calculator.

1. **49 + 82**

    Round 49 to _____ . Round 82 to _____ .

    The estimated sum is _____ + _____ = _____ .

    Calculator answer **49 + 82** _____

2. **92 + 69**

    Round 92 to _____ . Round 69 to _____ .

    The estimated sum is _____ + _____ = _____ .

    Calculator answer **92 + 69** _____

3. **697 + 921**

    Round 697 to _____ . Round 921 to _____ .

    The estimated sum is _____ + _____ = _____ .

    Calculator answer **697 + 921** _____

4. **401 + 837**

    Round 401 to _____ . Round 837 to _____ .

    The estimated sum is _____ + _____ = _____ .

    Calculator answer **401 + 837** _____

Name _____ Date _____

| Activity 2 |

Solve the word problems by rounding the numbers to the greatest place value. Then estimate the sums. Find the exact answers on a calculator and compare them.

Problem

There are 577 students in the 6th grade at Central Middle School. There are 621 students in the 7th grade. About how many students are there in both grades combined?

Estimate (rounding) _____ + _____ = _____

Exact Sum (exact numbers) _____ + _____ = _____

Comparison Are the two answers close to each other?

_____

Problem

Central is trying to figure out how many people buy lunch during 2nd and 3rd periods. Yesterday 122 students bought lunch during 2nd period, and 106 students bought lunch during 3rd period. About how many students bought lunch during 2nd and 3rd periods combined?

Estimate (rounding) _____ + _____ = _____

Exact Sum (exact numbers) _____ + _____ = _____

Comparison Are the two answers close to each other?

_____

Name _____ Date _____

 ## Problem-Solving Activity
Using Rounded Numbers in a Bar Graph

The table shows CD sales for The Moon Bandits. Use the table to create a bar graph of the data.

Before you make the graph, think about the following:

• How will each axis be labeled?

• What scale and interval will work best for the data?

• What happens if you choose a scale with an interval that is too large?

• What happens if you choose a scale with an interval that is too small?

Remember to think carefully about the scale and interval of the graph so that you can draw the bars accurately. Once you choose a scale and interval, use what you know about rounding to determine the height of each bar. Remember that the bars for CD sales will be between the numbers in the scale.

The Moon Bandits CD Sales for January–April	
Month	**CD Sales**
January	219
February	387
March	415
April	644

Name _____ Date _____

Title _____

mBook Reinforce Understanding
Use the *mBook Study Guide*
to review lesson concepts.

Unit 1 • Lesson 11 **35**

Name _____ Date _____

 Skills Maintenance
Extended Addition Facts

Activity 1

Complete the extended facts.

1. 60 + _____ = 110   **2.** _____ + 60 = 110   **3.** 40 + 90 = _____

4. _____ = 90 + 40   **5.** _____ + 50 = 120   **6.** 120 = _____ + 50

7. 130 = _____ + 80   **8.** 80 + _____ = 130   **9.** 170 = 90 + _____

Traditional Addition

Activity 2

Add using traditional addition.

1.   424
       + 283

2.   677
       + 99

3.   502
       + 198

Name _____ Date _____

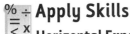 **Apply Skills**

Horizontal Expanded Addition

Activity 1

Find the sum of 37 and 42 using horizontal expanded addition.

$$
\begin{array}{cc}
37 & 30\,|\,7 \\
+\,42 & +\,40\,|\,2
\end{array}
$$

Step 1: Write the numbers in expanded form using an addition sign.

37 + 42 = _____ + _____ **+**_____ + _____

Step 2: Group the numbers together by place value.

37 + 42 = _____ + _____ **+**_____ + _____
             tens   *ones*

Step 3: Combine the place values to find the answer.

37 + 42 = _____ **+** _____
             tens   *ones*

Answer _____

Activity 2

Add using horizontal expanded addition. Write the sums in standard form.

1. 55 + 22 = _____

_____

_____

_____

2. 63 + 25 = _____

_____

_____

_____

3. 34 + 44 = _____

_____

_____

_____

4. 31 + 38 = _____

_____

_____

_____

Name _____ Date _____

Problem-Solving Activity
Horizontal Bar Graphs

Use the table to create a bar graph of the data.

José and his friends have tickets to see the Scatter Plots, but they need to decide the best way to get to the concert. They are going to meet at José's house. The table shows how long it takes to travel by three different modes of transportation.

Create a horizontal bar graph that shows this information. Make sure to put your labels in the right places.

Mode of Transportation	Time (in minutes)
Car	5
Bus	10
Foot	40

Title _____

mBook Reinforce Understanding
Use the *mBook Study Guide* to review lesson concepts.

Name _____ Date _____

 Skills Maintenance
Extended Addition Facts

Activity 1

Solve the extended facts.

1. 500 + 900 _____
2. 90 + 50 _____

3. 300 + 800 _____
4. 80 + 30 _____

5. 90 + 30 _____
6. 300 + 900 _____

7. 60 + 70 _____
8. 700 + 600 _____

Traditional Addition

Activity 2

Add using traditional addition.

1.
```
   952
 + 237
```

2.
```
   607
 +  78
```

3.
```
   819
 +  90
```

Name _____ Date _____

Apply Skills
Horizontal Addition With Hundreds

Activity 1

Add using horizontal expanded addition.

1.   437 + 42 = _____ + _____ + _____   +   _____ + _____

_____   +   _____ + _____   +   _____ + _____
hundreds   *tens*   *ones*

_____   +   _____   +   _____
hundreds   *tens*   *ones*

Answer _____

2.   123 + 410 = _____ + _____ + _____   +   _____ + _____ + _____

_____ + _____   +   _____ + _____   +   _____ + _____
hundreds   *tens*   *ones*

_____   +   _____   +   _____
hundreds   *tens*   *ones*

Answer _____

Name _____ Date _____

Problem-Solving Activity
Collecting Data and Constructing Graphs

Complete the steps:

1. Survey the class by asking each classmate the same question. Include three or four possible responses for them to choose from.

2. Use a lined sheet of paper to create a table for the data. List the question that was asked at the top of the table, and make sure each column has a heading.

3. Record your classmates' responses in the table. Mark a tally in the appropriate row for each response, and then total the tally marks when at least 10 of your classmates have been surveyed.

4. Use the table to create a bar graph for the data. Make sure your graph includes a title, labels for each axis, and an appropriate scale and interval. You have the option to create either a vertical or a horizontal graph.

Title _____

mBook Reinforce Understanding
Use the *mBook Study Guide*
to review lesson concepts.

Name _____ Date _____

Skills Maintenance
Basic and Extended Addition Facts

Activity 1

Complete the basic and extended facts.

1. 9 + _____ = 11   90 + _____ = 110   900 + _____ = 1,100

2. 8 + _____ = 14   80 + _____ = 140   800 + _____ = 1,400

3. _____ + 7 = 15   _____ + 70 = 150   _____ + 700 = 1,500

4. 5 + 6 = _____   50 + 60 = _____   600 + 500 = _____

Traditional Addition

Activity 2

Add using traditional addition.

1.   743   2.   628   3.   555
    + 79   + 191   + 266

Name _____ Date _____

Problem-Solving Activity
Creating a Pictograph

Create a pictograph that shows the data in the table. As you create the pictograph, remember to think about:

- Choose an icon that is appropriate to show the number of tickets sold, such as a ticket stub.
- Choose a value for the icon that represents the data as accurately as possible. Make sure to include this information in the key of the pictograph.

One Later Ticket Sales	
City	**Number of Tickets Sold**
Phoenix	700
Denver	550
Austin	385
Chicago	915

key

mBook Reinforce Understanding
Use the *mBook Study Guide*
to review lesson concepts.

Name _____ Date _____

 ## Skills Maintenance
Basic and Extended Addition Facts

Activity 1

Complete the basic and extended fact families.

1. $9 +$ _____ $= 15$

   $90 +$ _____ $= 150$

   $900 +$ _____ $= 1,500$

2. _____ $+ 7 = 12$

   _____ $+ 70 = 120$

   _____ $+ 700 = 1,200$

3. $8 +$ _____ $= 16$

   $80 +$ _____ $= 160$

   $800 +$ _____ $= 1,600$

4. $7 + 6 =$ _____

   $70 + 60 =$ _____

   $700 + 600 =$ _____

Expanded Addition

Activity 2

Add using expanded addition. Then write the answers in standard form.

1.
```
   31
+ 42
```

Answer _____

2.
```
  537
+ 61
```

Answer _____

3.
```
  325
+ 214
```

Answer _____

Name _____ Date _____

 Unit Review
Addition

Activity 1

Add using horizontal expanded addition. Write the answers in standard form.

1. 28 + 61 = _____ + _____   +   _____ + _____
                    tens   *ones*

    _____   +   _____
      tens   *ones*

    Answer _____

2. 37 + 22 = _____ + _____   +   _____ + _____
                    tens   *ones*

    _____   +   _____
      tens   *ones*

    Answer _____

3. 152 + 35 = _____ + _____ + _____   +   _____ + _____

    _____   +   _____ + _____   +   _____ + _____
     hundreds   *tens*   *ones*

    _____   +   _____   +   _____
     hundreds   *tens*   *ones*

    Answer _____

Name _____ Date _____

Activity 2

Estimate the numbers represented by the dot on the number lines.

1.
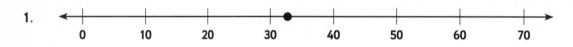

_____

2.

_____

Activity 3

Use the number lines to estimate the sums. Then find the exact sums.

1. 11 + 59   2. 38 + 64

_____   _____

_____   _____

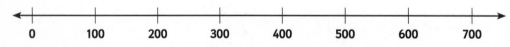

3. 387 + 421   4. 501 + 211

_____   _____

_____   _____

Activity 4

Add using traditional addition.

1.   444   2.   707   3.   121
    + 79   + 93   + 379

Name _____ Date _____

Unit Review
Working With Data

Activity 1

Read each problem carefully. Decide what the problem is asking for.

Problem

To get into a world record book for bicycling, you would need to ride a bike faster than 60 mph. Toby likes to race with his bike. He thinks he is pretty fast. During his last race, he wondered if he was riding fast enough to get into a world record book. It took him one hour to finish the race. The distance of the race was 20 miles. He was tired after the race.

1. What is the problem asking for?

    _____

    _____

Problem

Each day the world population increases by about 240,000 people. Half the world's population lives in just six countries. Many people in the world live in just one country—China. Many of the countries with large populations are very poor, and there is a great deal of illness. About how much does the world population increase every week?

2. What is the problem asking for?

    _____

    _____

Name _____ Date _____

Activity 2

Use the bar graph to answer the questions. The bar graph shows attendance at the citywide basketball tournament held every year at Meadow Park. It shows the number of people who watched the tournament on different days.

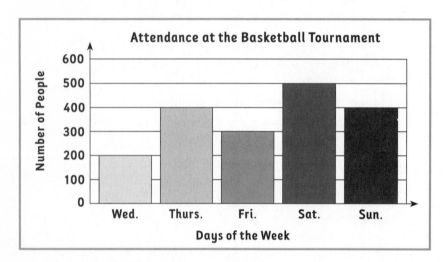

1. What day had the most attendance?

   _____

2. How many more people came to the tournament on Sunday than on Friday?

   _____

3. What was the total attendance for Saturday and Sunday?

   _____

Name _____ Date _____

Activity 3

Use the pictograph to answer the questions.

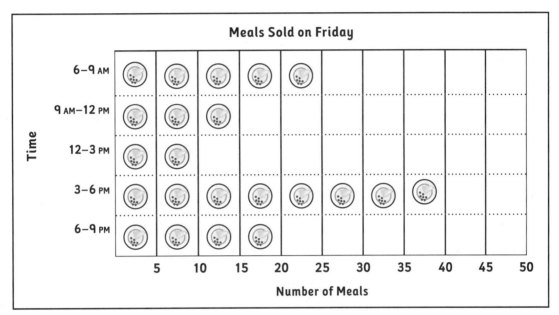

key
= 5 meals

1. What time of day had the most meals sold?

   _____

2. How many more meals were sold from 6 PM to 9 PM than from 9 AM to 12 PM?

   _____

3. What was the total number of meals sold from 3 PM to 9 PM?

   _____

mBook **Reinforce Understanding**
Use the *mBook Study Guide*
to review lesson concepts.

Name _____ Date _____

 Skills Maintenance
Basic and Extended Addition Facts

Activity 1

Complete the sets of basic and extended addition facts.

1. 7 + 2 = _____   20 + 70 = _____   700 + 200 = _____

2. 3 + _____ = 9   _____ + 30 = 90   30 + _____ = 90

3. 9 + 3 = _____   90 + 30 = _____   900 + 300 = _____

4. 4 + 7 = _____   40 + 70 = _____   700 + 400 = _____

5. 8 + 1 = _____   80 + 10 = _____   800 + 100 = _____

Name _____ Date _____

%÷ Apply Skills
Addition and Subtraction Fact Families

Activity 1

Write the basic fact families for the groups of numbers.

1. 7, 8, and 15

_____ + _____ = _____

_____ + _____ = _____

_____ − _____ = _____

_____ − _____ = _____

2. 6, 7, and 13

_____ + _____ = _____

_____ + _____ = _____

_____ − _____ = _____

_____ − _____ = _____

Activity 2

Complete the subtraction facts using related addition facts.

1. $14 - 6 =$ _____   **2.** $11 - 5 =$ _____   **3.** $8 - 3 =$ _____

4. $10 - 7 =$ _____   **5.** $17 - 8 =$ _____   **6.** $9 - 6 =$ _____

Activity 3

Write the extended fact families for the groups of numbers.

1. 70, 80, and 150

_____ + _____ = _____

_____ + _____ = _____

_____ − _____ = _____

_____ − _____ = _____

2. 20, 90, and 110

_____ + _____ = _____

_____ + _____ = _____

_____ − _____ = _____

_____ − _____ = _____

Unit 2

Name _____ Date _____

 ## Problem-Solving Activity
Answering the Right Question

The Civic Auditorium hired the Scatter Plots to play a concert last Friday. The table lists the cost for each concert expense. Use the data to solve the problems. Show all your work. Remember to check your answer by asking yourself, "Did I answer the question asked in the problem?"

Expense	Cost
Security	$200
Stage crew	$300
Lighting and sound	$100
Concessions (food and drink)	$120
Standard employees	$700
Total	$1,420

1. It was expensive to put on the concert. The Civic Auditorium had to pay for security, a stage crew, lighting and sound, concessions, and the standard employees who take tickets and clean up. How much more did the standard employees cost than security for the concert?

_____

_____

2. The owners of the Civic Auditorium had to figure out how much to pay the Scatter Plots. They decided to pay them $900. How much more did they pay the Scatter Plots than the stage crew?

_____

_____

3. Auditorium owners make money at a concert through concession sales—selling food and drinks. The Civic Auditorium bought food and drinks to sell at the concert. The concession sales for the Scatter Plots' concert were $240. How much profit did the owners make on concessions? The profit is the difference between how much money was spent buying the food and drinks and how much money was made selling the food and drinks.

_____

_____

Name _____ Date _____

 Skills Maintenance
Basic and Extended Fact Families

Activity 1

Find the missing values for the basic fact families.

1. 7 + 8 = _____

    8 + 7 = _____

    _____ − 7 = 8

    _____ − 8 = 7

2. 6 + 9 = _____

    9 + 6 = _____

    _____ − 6 = 9

    _____ − 9 = 6

3. _____ + 6 = 13

    6 + _____ = 13

    13 − 6 = _____

    13 − _____ = 6

Activity 2

Write the extended fact families for the groups of numbers.

1. 70, 80, and 150

    _____ + _____ = _____

    _____ + _____ = _____

    _____ − _____ = _____

    _____ − _____ = _____

2. 200, 900, and 1,100

    _____ + _____ = _____

    _____ + _____ = _____

    _____ − _____ = _____

    _____ − _____ = _____

Name _____ Date _____

 Apply Skills
Expanded Subtraction

Activity 1

Write the subtraction problems in expanded form and solve.

1. 69
    − 27   Answer _____

2. 57
    − 36   Answer _____

3. 96
    − 32   Answer _____

4. 597
    − 175   Answer _____

5. 358
    − 142   Answer _____

Name _____ Date _____

Problem-Solving Activity
Analyzing Data Using Subtraction

Use the bar graph to answer the questions. Write an extended fact to solve each problem.

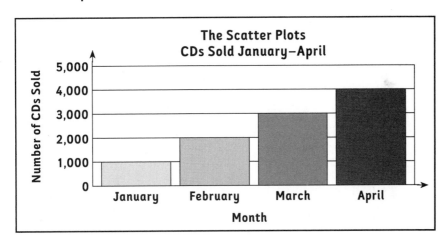

The Scatter Plots
CDs Sold January–April

1. What is the difference between the number of CDs the Scatter Plots sold in March and the number they sold in April?

   _____

   _____

2. What is the difference in sales between January and February?

   _____

   _____

3. What is the difference in sales between February and April?

   _____

   _____

4. If this pattern of sales continues, how many CDs would be sold in the month of May?

   _____

   _____

mBook Reinforce Understanding
Use the mBook *Study Guide* to review lesson concepts.

Name _____ Date _____

Skills Maintenance
Basic and Extended Fact Families

Activity 1

Find the missing values for the basic and extended fact families.

1. 5 + 6 = _____

    6 + 5 = _____

    _____ − 6 = 5

    _____ − 5 = 6

2. 50 + 60 = _____

    60 + 50 = _____

    _____ − 60 = 50

    _____ − 50 = 60

3. 600 + 500 = _____

    500 + 600 = _____

    _____ − 600 = 500

    _____ − 500 = 600

Name _____ Date _____

 Apply Skills
Expanded Subtraction With Regrouping

Activity 1

Write the problems in expanded form and solve. Show the regrouping step.

1. 75
   − 59 → ___|___ ___|___ Answer _____

2. 82
   − 77 → ___|___ ___|___ Answer _____

3. 52
   − 37 → ___|___ ___|___ Answer _____

4. 24 →
   − 7   ___|___ ___|___ Answer _____

Name _____ Date _____

Problem-Solving Activity
Locating Information in a Table

The table contains information about cities on the Scatter Plots' concert tour. Use the table to answer the questions.

Cities on the Scatter Plots' Tour			
City Name	Population	Number of Concerts	Average Attendance
New York City	8,143,197	4	5,000
Indianapolis	784,118	2	2,000
Miami	386,417	1	1,000
Dallas	1,213,825	3	3,000
Phoenix	1,461,575	3	3,500
Tulsa	382,457	1	800

1. In what city did the Scatter Plots perform the most number of concerts?

   _____

2. Which city on the tour has the smallest population?

   _____

3. How much more was the average attendance at the Scatter Plots' concerts in Phoenix than Miami?

   _____

4. How many concerts did the Scatter Plots perform during its tour?

   _____

5. Which city had an average attendance of 3,000 people per concert?

   _____

mBook Reinforce Understanding
Use the mBook *Study Guide* to review lesson concepts.

Name _____ Date _____

 ## Skills Maintenance
Extended Fact Families

Activity 1

Find the missing values for each fact family.

1. $70 + 90 =$ _____

    $90 + 70 =$ _____

    _____ $- 90 = 70$

    _____ $- 70 = 90$

2. $600 + 800 =$ _____

    $800 + 600 =$ _____

    _____ $- 60 = 80$

    _____ $- 80 = 60$

3. _____ $+ 5{,}000 = 12{,}000$

    $5{,}000 +$ _____ $= 12{,}000$

    $12{,}000 - 5{,}000 =$ _____

    $12{,}000 -$ _____ $= 5{,}000$

Name _____ Date _____

 Apply Skills
Regrouping in Subtraction

Activity 1

Write the problems in expanded form and solve.

1.   352
   − 181   →

   Answer _____

2.   912
   − 783   →

   Answer _____

3.   425
   − 158   →

   Answer _____

Name _____ Date _____

 Problem-Solving Activity
Working With Tables and Graphs

Hipster Records researched the number of rock, country, and pop CDs bought by consumers last month. Hipster used the data it found to create the bar graph.

Use it to create a table that shows the same data. Remember to label the columns in the table. Then determine the total number of CDs that were bought by consumers last month.

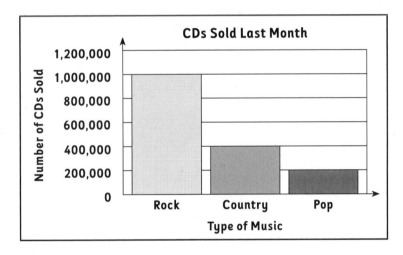

_____

_____

mBook Reinforce Understanding
Use the mBook *Study Guide* to review lesson concepts.

Name _____ Date _____

Skills Maintenance
Extended Fact Families

Activity 1

Find the missing values for the fact families.

1. $90 + 80 =$ _____

    $80 + 90 =$ _____

    _____ $- 90 = 80$

    _____ $- 80 = 90$

2. $600 + 900 =$ _____

    $900 + 600 =$ _____

    _____ $- 600 = 900$

    _____ $- 900 = 600$

3. _____ $+ 6,000 = 13,000$

    $6,000 +$ _____ $= 13,000$

    $13,000 - 6,000 =$ _____

    $13,000 -$ _____ $= 6,000$

Reading Bar Graphs

Activity 2

The bar graph shows the amount of money spent on Internet, radio, and TV in one year. Use the bar graph to solve the problem.

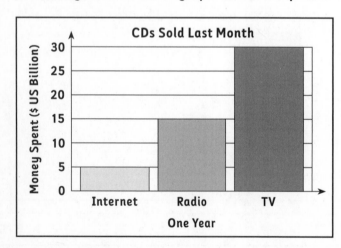

1. What was the difference in money spent on advertising for TV and radio?

    _____

Name _____ Date _____

%÷ Apply Skills
≤× Traditional Subtraction

Activity 1

Solve using expanded subtraction. Then write the answer in standard form.

1. 52
   − 18   →   ___|___   ___|___   Answer _____

Activity 2

Find the differences using traditional subtraction.

1. 52
   − 18   Answer _____

2. 91
   − 43   Answer _____

Activity 3

Describe the biggest difference between expanded and traditional subtraction.

_____

_____

_____

_____

_____

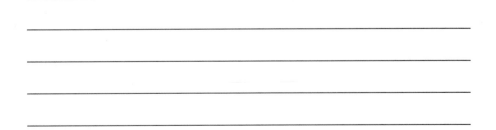 **mBook** **Reinforce Understanding**
Use the mBook *Study Guide* to review lesson concepts.

Name _____ Date _____

 Skills Maintenance
Expanded Subtraction

Activity 1

Solve using expanded subtraction. Then write the answers in standard form.

1. 28
    − 16   Answer _____

2. 367
    − 153      Answer _____

3. 589
    − 372      Answer _____

Apply Skills
Estimating Differences

Name _____ Date _____

Activity 1

Estimate the differences. Then use a calculator to compute the exact answers and compare them.

$$56$$
$$-\ 17$$

1. We round 56 to _____ .

2. We round 17 to _____ .

3. The extended equation is _____ − 20 = 40.

4. The estimated answer is _____ .

5. The exact answer is _____ .

6. How does your estimate compare to the exact answer? Explain.

_____

_____

_____

_____

_____

Name _____ Date _____

Problem-Solving Activity
Finding Distances on a Map

The Scatter Plots is on a countrywide tour. Right now, the five-member group is performing in Pittsburgh. Tomorrow the group must drive to Philadelphia. Two of the members want to go through Clarion, Williamsport, and Allentown, and the other three members want to travel through Harrisburg. Use the map and table to answer the questions.

Driving Distances Between Cities in Pennsylvania	
Cities	Distance (in miles)
Pittsburgh to Harrisburg	164
Pittsburgh to Clarion	66
Clarion to Williamsport	118
Williamsport to Allentown	91
Harrisburg to Philadelphia	90
Allentown to Philadelphia	48

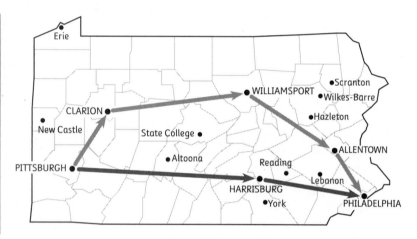

1. About how far is it to go from Pittsburgh, through Clarion, Williamsport, and Allentown, to Philadelphia? Use quarter rounding.

    _____

2. About how far is it to go from Pittsburgh through Harrisburg to Philadelphia? Use quarter rounding.

    _____

3. About how much farther is the route through Clarion, Williamsport, and Allentown than the route through Harrisburg?

    _____

mBook Reinforce Understanding
Use the mBook *Study Guide* to review lesson concepts.

Name _____ Date _____

 Skills Maintenance
Addition and Subtraction

Activity 1

Find the missing values for the fact families.

1. 7 + 9 = _____

    9 + 7 = _____

    _____ − 7 = 9

    _____ − 9 = 7

2. 70 + 90 = _____

    90 + 70 = _____

    _____ − 70 = 90

    _____ − 90 = 70

3. 25 + 75 = _____

    75 + 25 = _____

    _____ − 25 = 75

    _____ − 75 = 25

Activity 2

Find the differences using traditional subtraction.

1.   56
   − 19

2.   310
   − 41

3.   274
   − 165

Name _____ Date _____

 Apply Skills
Estimating to Check Answers

Activity 1

Solve the problems using traditional subtraction, then check the answers using estimation.

Problem	Answer	Estimate

1. 797
   − 192
   _____

2. 399
   − 201
   _____

3. 454
   − 227
   _____

4. 891
   − 699
   _____

5. 779
   − 124
   _____

Name _____ Date _____

Unit 2

 ## Problem-Solving Activity
Checking Answers in Word Problems

Solve the word problems using a calculator and estimation. Write both answers on your paper. Use the estimates to check the calculator answers. If the numbers are not close, try to find the errors and fix them. Write about any errors you discover using estimation.

1. The Scatter Plots went on a concert tour last summer. It visited 20 cities. The attendance for the first 10 cities was 15,612 and for the last 10 cities was 12,999. What was the difference?

   _____

   _____

   _____

   _____

2. C U Later also toured last summer. It had a total attendance of 11,223 at its concerts. What was the attendance figure for the last concert? The total attendance for its first 11 concerts was 9,899.

   _____

   _____

   _____

   _____

mBook Reinforce Understanding
Use the mBook *Study Guide* to review lesson concepts.

Name _____ Date _____

 Skills Maintenance
Fact Families

Activity 1

Complete the quarter facts. Think of the quarters you use for money to help.

1. $75 - 25 =$ _____
2. $100 -$ _____ $= 50$
3. $75 +$ _____ $= 100$

4. $25 + 50 =$ _____
5. _____ $- 25 = 75$
6. $100 + 25 =$ _____

7. $225 - 25 =$ _____
8. $150 +$ _____ $= 200$
9. $350 -$ _____ $= 300$

Traditional Subtraction

Activity 2

Find the differences using traditional subtraction.

1. $\begin{array}{r} 52 \\ -27 \\ \hline \end{array}$

2. $\begin{array}{r} 764 \\ -\ 83 \\ \hline \end{array}$

3. $\begin{array}{r} 852 \\ -427 \\ \hline \end{array}$

Name _____ Date _____

Apply Skills
Quarter Rounding

Activity 1

Label the numbers on the number lines and round them to the nearest quarter.

1. Where is 105? What is the nearest quarter? _____

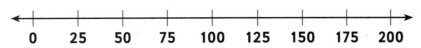

2. Where is 160? What is the nearest quarter? _____

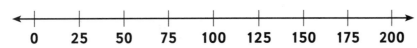

3. Where is 195? What is the nearest quarter? _____

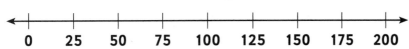

4. Where is 29? What is the nearest quarter? _____

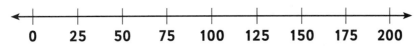

5. Where is 109? What is the nearest quarter? _____

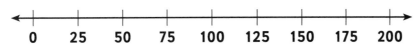

Activity 2

Estimate the difference by quarter rounding. Then find the difference using traditional subtraction and compare.

1. $\begin{array}{r} 68 \\ -48 \\ \hline \end{array}$ 2. $\begin{array}{r} 97 \\ -23 \\ \hline \end{array}$ 3. $\begin{array}{r} 42 \\ -19 \\ \hline \end{array}$

Name _____ Date _____

Problem-Solving Activity
Estimating in Word Problems

The Scatter Plots just finished its concerts in Pennsylvania, and the group is about to fly to Florida for its next concert. The group's manager tells the band members that it made a profit of $4,537 from the concerts in Pennsylvania. The drummer, Tim, is angry. He says "No way! We made over $3,000 in both Pittsburgh and Philadelphia! That is over $6,000!"

The manager calms Tim down and explains that he had to subtract the band's expenses from its income to determine the profit. Tim still wants to find out if the manager calculated the profit correctly.

Help Tim calculate the Scatter Plots' profit. Use a calculator. Compare your value to the one the manager found. Was the manager correct?

Income		Expenses	
Payment for two Pittsburgh concerts	$3,250	Hotel rooms in Pittsburgh (two nights)	$478
Payment for two Philadelphia concerts	$3,600	Hotel rooms in Philadelphia (two nights)	$461
		Food for the time spent in Pennsylvania	$986
		Rental cars and gas for the time spent in Pennsylvania	$294
		Miscellaneous expenses	$94

_____

_____

_____

_____

_____

mBook Reinforce Understanding
Use the mBook *Study Guide* to review lesson concepts.

Name _____ Date _____

 Skills Maintenance
Basic and Extended Fact Families

Activity 1

Find the missing values for the fact families.

1. 4 + 8 = _____   8 + 4 = _____   _____ − 8 = 4   _____ − 4 = 8

2. 40 + 80 = _____   80 + 40 = _____   _____ − 80 = 40   _____ − 40 = 80

3. 6 + 7 = _____   7 + 6 = _____   _____ − 7 = 6   _____ − 6 = 7

4. 60 + 70 = _____   70 + 60 = _____   _____ − 70 = 60   _____ − 60 = 70

Name _____ Date _____

Apply Skills
More Estimating Differences

Activity 1

Estimate the differences. Then use a calculator to compute the exact answers and compare them.

1.   3,056
     − 1,917

We round 3,056 to _____ .

We round 1,917 to _____ .

The extended fact is _____ − 2,000 = 1,000.

The estimated answer is _____ .

With the calculator, the exact answer is _____ .

2.   4,001
     − 3,078

We round 4,001 to _____ .

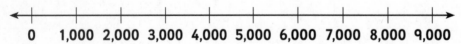

We round 3,078 to _____ .

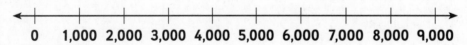

The extended fact is _____ − 3,000 = 1,000.

The estimated answer is _____ .

With the calculator, the exact answer is _____ .

Name _____ Date _____

Problem-Solving Activity
Using Estimation to Check a Bill

The Scatter Plots decided it was time to replace some of its older music equipment and instruments. They wanted to replace a microphone, an amplifier, two guitar cords, a bass guitar, an electric guitar, and a snare drum. The group stopped at a small music store in a nearby town.

The music store clerk priced the equipment:
    Microphone: $321
    Amplifier: $470
    Two guitar cords: $89

Then the clerk priced the instruments:
    Bass guitar: $982
    Electric guitar: $1,078
    Snare drum: $2,868

The clerk said, "The total cost for the equipment will be $880 plus tax. The total cost for the instruments will be $4,928 plus tax."

Was the music store clerk correct? Estimate the total bill for the music equipment and instruments. Explain your answer.

_____

_____

_____

_____

_____

_____

_____

_____

_____

mBook Reinforce Understanding
Use the mBook *Study Guide* to review lesson concepts.

Name _____ Date _____

 ## Skills Maintenance
Basic and Extended Fact Families

Activity 1

Find the missing values for the fact families.

1. $4 + 9 =$ _____ $9 + 4 =$ _____   _____ $- 4 = 9$ _____ $- 9 = 4$

2. $40 + 90 =$ _____ $90 + 40 =$ _____   _____ $- 40 = 90$ _____ $- 90 = 40$

3. $6 + 5 =$ _____ $5 + 6 =$ _____   _____ $- 5 = 6$ _____ $- 6 = 5$

4. $60 + 50 =$ _____ $50 + 60 =$ _____   _____ $- 50 = 60$ _____ $- 60 = 50$

Quarter Rounding

Activity 2

Round the numbers in the table to the nearest quarter to solve the problem.

Votes for Town Candidates in the November Election				
Johnson	Curtis	Rodriguez	Lee	O'Brien
479	997	1,000	917	556

1. About how many more votes did Rodriguez receive than Lee?

    _____

2. About how many votes did Lee and Curtis receive together?

    _____

3. About how many more votes did O'Brien receive than Johnson?

    _____

Name _____ Date _____

 Apply Skills
Common Subtraction Errors

Activity 1

Each problem contains an error. Use expanded form to find and fix the errors.

1.   896
    − 248   →   ⊞   ⊞   Answer _____

2.   601
    − 240   →   ⊞   ⊞   Answer _____

Activity 2

Describe the errors in the problems in Activity 1.

_____

_____

_____

_____

_____

_____

_____

_____

_____

_____

 mBook Reinforce Understanding
Use the mBook *Study Guide* to review lesson concepts.

Name _____ Date _____

 Skills Maintenance
Traditional Subtraction

Activity 1

Find the differences using traditional subtraction.

1. 157
    − 28
    _____

2. 428
    − 51
    _____

3. 861
    −219
    _____

4. 532
    −341
    _____

Name _____ Date _____

Apply Skills
Using Addition to Check Subtraction

Activity 1

Use addition to check the answers to the subtraction problems. If the answer is incorrect, use expanded subtraction to find the correct answer.

1. 585
   − 206   →

   Answer _____

2. 843
   − 785   →

   Answer _____

Name _____ Date _____

 Problem-Solving Activity

Understanding Income, Expenses, and Profit

Use the table to answer the questions about the Scatter Plots' expenses for its tour.

The Scatter Plots' Summer Tour Income and Expenses			
Concert Location	**Income**	**Expense Item**	**Cost**
		Airline tickets to the different states	$5,115
Pennsylvania		Pennsylvania	
4 concerts	$9,850	Rental Car	$294
		Food	$986
		Hotels	$939
Florida		Florida	
4 concerts	$10,965	Rental Car	$314
		Food	$1,089
		Hotels	$1,098
Texas		Texas	
4 concerts	$9,266	Motor Home	$1,042
		Food	$1,545
		Hotels	$612

1. Compute the band's profit for Florida.

    _____

    _____

2. How much more did the band pay for food than hotels in Pennsylvania?

    _____

3. What was the total income for the Scatter Plots' summer tour?

    _____

    _____

 mBook Reinforce Understanding

Use the mBook *Study Guide* to review lesson concepts.

Name _____ Date _____

 Skills Maintenance
Basic and Extended Fact Families

Activity 1

Find the missing values for the basic and extended fact families.

1. 7 + 8 = _____

    8 + 7 = _____

    _____ − 7 = 8

    _____ − 8 = 7

2. 70 + 80 = _____

    80 + 70 = _____

    _____ − 70 = 80

    _____ − 80 = 70

3. 2 + 9 = _____

    9 + 2 = _____

    _____ − 2 = 9

    _____ − 9 = 2

4. 200 + 900 = _____

    900 + 200 = _____

    _____ − 200 = 900

    _____ − 900 = 200

Unit 2

Name _____ Date _____

Apply Skills
Zeros in Subtraction

Activity 1

Solve the problems using traditional or expanded subtraction. Then use estimation and a calculator to check the answers.

1.   302   or
    − 143

Answer _____

Estimation _____ − 150 = 150

Calculator Check _____

2.   8,001   or
    −6,233

Answer _____

Estimation _____ − 6,250 = 1,750

Calculator Check _____

3.   6,002   or
    −1,043

Answer _____

Estimation _____ − 1,050 = 4,950

Calculator Check _____

Name _____ Date _____

📝 Problem-Solving Activity
Understanding Budgets

Look at the map that shows the Scatter Plots' route across Texas and the table that shows the driving distances between cities. Use the map and table to answer the questions below. Show all your work.

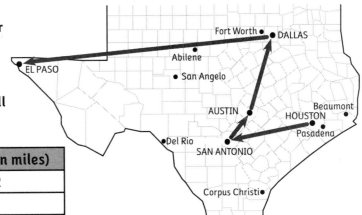

Texas Cities	Distance (in miles)
Houston to San Antonio	182
San Antonio to Austin	68
Austin to Dallas	176
Dallas to El Paso	569

1. Did the Scatter Plots drive more or less than 1,000 miles from Houston to El Paso? Use a calculator to find how far the group drove.

    _____

    _____

2. On the part of the trip from Austin to Dallas to El Paso, did the Scatter Plots travel more than 800 miles? Explain how you know.

    _____

    _____

    _____

    _____

mBook Reinforce Understanding
Use the mBook *Study Guide* to review lesson concepts.

Name _____ Date _____

 ### Skills Maintenance
Subtraction With the Numbers 1 and 5

Activity 1

Solve the subtraction problems.

1. $10 - 9 =$ _____ $100 - 99 =$ _____ $1,000 - 999 =$ _____

2. $10 - 5 =$ _____ $100 - 95 =$ _____ $1,000 - 995 =$ _____

3. $10 - 1 =$ _____ $100 - 1 =$ _____ $1,000 - 1 =$ _____

4. $10 - 5 =$ _____ $100 - 5 =$ _____ $1,000 - 5 =$ _____

Traditional Subtraction

Activity 2

Find the differences using traditional subtraction.

1.   80   2.   602   3.   740   4.   203
    $- 27$ $- 391$ $- 135$ $- 142$

Name _____ Date _____

 Apply Skills
Good Number Sense

Activity 1

Solve the problems using good number sense and mental math.

1.   500
     − 299

2.   500
     − 302

3.   700
     − 495

4.   700
     − 505

Name _____ Date _____

 Problem-Solving Activity
Solving With Estimation

Solve the problems using estimation alone.

1. Ajax works part-time at the grocery store after school. The first
    month of school he made $290, and the second month of school he
    made $350. Ajax wants to buy a racing bike for $750. Did he make
    enough money in the first two months of school to buy it?

    (a) Can you solve the problem using estimation?

    _____

    (b) Explain why.

    _____

    _____

2. Ajax works a third month, but he has a lot of homework, so he
    doesn't get many hours in. He makes only $105 the third month.
    Does he have enough now to buy the racing bike?

    (a) Can you solve the problem using estimation?

    _____

    (b) Explain why.

    _____

    _____

    _____

    _____

mBook Reinforce Understanding
Use the mBook *Study Guide* to review lesson concepts.

Name _____ Date _____

Skills Maintenance
Fact Families With Quarter Facts

Activity 1

Write the fact families for the groups of numbers.

1. 25, 75, and Z

2. 250, Z, and 750

_____ + _____ = _____   _____ + _____ = _____

_____ + _____ = _____   _____ + _____ = _____

_____ − _____ = _____   _____ − _____ = _____

_____ − _____ = _____   _____ − _____ = _____

Traditional Subtraction

Activity 2

Find the differences using traditional subtraction.

1. 700
    − 103

2. 891
    − 134

3. 205
    − 109

Name _____ Date _____

 Apply Skills
Writing About What We Learned

Activity 1

Choose the best method for solving each problem. Then explain your thinking and solve the problems.

1.   4,905   Method: (circle one)
    − 1,896   **(a)** Traditional Subtraction
                (b) Estimation and a Calculator
                (c) Mental Math

Explain your thinking _____

_____

_____

2.   500   Method: (circle one)
    − 198   **(a)** Traditional Subtraction
               (b) Estimation and a Calculator
               (c) Mental Math

Explain your thinking _____

_____

_____

3.   257   Method: (circle one)
    − 145   **(a)** Traditional Subtraction
               (b) Estimation and a Calculator
               (c) Mental Math

Explain your thinking _____

_____

_____

Name _____ Date _____

Problem-Solving Activity
Writing Good Word Problems

The table shows how a popular movie did in theaters for the first 10 weeks of its release. For each week, it shows how much the movie made at the box office and the number of theaters where it played.

Write three word problems using information from the table, and provide an answer for each problem. Look for trends in the data that occurred over the 10 weeks to help you write the problems.

Week	Box Office Receipts	Number of Theaters
1	$57 million	3,587
2	$64 million	3,623
3	$39 million	3,661
4	$25 million	3,715
5	$21 million	3,317
6	$16 million	3,007
7	$14 million	2,704
8	$9 million	2,107
9	$6 million	1,767
10	$4 million	1,551

_____

_____

_____

_____

_____

_____

_____

mBook Reinforce Understanding
Use the mBook *Study Guide* to review lesson concepts.

Name _____ Date _____

 Skills Maintenance
Traditional Subtraction

Activity 1

Solve the traditional subtraction problems.

1.
$$\begin{array}{r} 485 \\ -225 \\ \hline \end{array}$$

2.
$$\begin{array}{r} 375 \\ -225 \\ \hline \end{array}$$

3.
$$\begin{array}{r} 150 \\ -\ 75 \\ \hline \end{array}$$

4.
$$\begin{array}{r} 625 \\ -322 \\ \hline \end{array}$$

5.
$$\begin{array}{r} 2,000 \\ -\ 1,995 \\ \hline \end{array}$$

6.
$$\begin{array}{r} 980 \\ -150 \\ \hline \end{array}$$

7.
$$\begin{array}{r} 10,001 \\ -\ \ \ 999 \\ \hline \end{array}$$

8.
$$\begin{array}{r} 123 \\ -\ 79 \\ \hline \end{array}$$

9.
$$\begin{array}{r} 5,472 \\ -\ \ \ 384 \\ \hline \end{array}$$

10.
$$\begin{array}{r} 15,000 \\ -14,975 \\ \hline \end{array}$$

11.
$$\begin{array}{r} 9,998 \\ -9,990 \\ \hline \end{array}$$

12.
$$\begin{array}{r} 784 \\ -165 \\ \hline \end{array}$$

Name _____ Date _____

 Unit Review
Subtraction

Activity 1

Solve the basic and extended quarter fact families.

1. $25 + 50 =$ _____

   $50 \div 25 =$ _____

   _____ $- 25 = 50$

   _____ $- 50 = 25$

2. $250 + 500 =$ _____

   $500 + 250 =$ _____

   _____ $- 250 = 500$

   _____ $- 500 = 250$

3. $25 +$ _____ $= 125$

   _____ $+ 25 = 125$

   $125 - 25 =$ _____

   $125 -$ _____ $= 25$

Activity 2

Solve using expanded subtraction.

1. $\begin{array}{r} 67 \\ -\,32 \end{array}$ →  Answer _____

2. $\begin{array}{r} 776 \\ -\,223 \end{array}$ →  Answer _____

Activity 3

Decide whether to use front-end rounding or rounding to the nearest quarter. Estimate the answers. Then find the actual answers with your calculator.

Problem	Rounding Strategy	Estimate	Calculator Answer
1. $\begin{array}{r} 251 \\ -\,179 \end{array}$			
2. $\begin{array}{r} 401 \\ -\,299 \end{array}$			

Unit 2

Name _____ Date _____

Activity 4

Solve using any method.

1.   86
   − 27

2.   464
   − 93

3.   819
   − 427

4.   982
   − 376

Activity 5

Some of the problems contain errors. Circle the errors and fix them.

1.   ^{3 15}
   4̶2̶
  − 27
    15

2.   ^{3 16}
   4̶6̶4̶
  − 93
   431

3.   ^{7 11}
   8̶1̶9̶
  − 427
   392

4.   ^{7 12}
   9̶8̶2̶
  − 376
   506

Activity 6

Choose the best method to solve the problems.
The choices are:
    (a) Traditional Subtraction
    (b) Estimation and Calculator
    (c) Good Number Sense and Number Line

Then solve.

1.   4,905   Method _____
   − 1,896

2.   600   Method _____
   − 395

3.   874   Method _____
   − 526

Name _____ Date _____

Unit Review
Working With Data

Activity 1

Use the map and key to answer the questions.

Travel (from where to where)	Distance (in miles)
From San Francisco, CA to Eugene, OR	310
From Los Angeles, CA to San Francisco, CA	303
From Eugene, OR to Seattle, WA	247
From Walla Walla, WA to Portland, OR	213
From Santa Cruz, CA to San Diego, CA	404

1. How many miles would it be if you traveled from Los Angeles, CA to Eugene, OR?

2. You traveled from Eugene, OR to Seattle, WA. There was a detour for 37 miles because of a tractor-trailer accident. But it saved you 26 miles in distance. How many miles did you travel?

3. On the road from Santa Cruz to San Diego, you decided to stop at Mission Santa Barbara. You traveled 7 miles into the city of Santa Barbara before you realized that you were going the wrong way. You drove another 12 miles in the other direction to reach the mission. Then you had to drive 3 miles back to the highway. What is your mileage for this side trip?

mBook Reinforce Understanding
Use the mBook *Study Guide* to review lesson concepts.

Name _____ Date _____

 ## Skills Maintenance
Basic Multiplication Facts

Activity 1

Complete the basic multiplication facts.

1. $3 \times 9 =$ _____

2. $9 \times 3 =$ _____

3. $3 \times$ _____ $= 27$

4. $8 \times 9 =$ _____

5. $9 \times 8 =$ _____

6. $6 \times$ _____ $= 42$

7. $7 \times$ _____ $= 42$

8. _____ $\times 9 = 36$

9. _____ $\times 4 = 36$

Name _____ Date _____

Apply Skills
Basic and Extended Multiplication Facts

Activity 1

Write three extended facts for each of the basic multiplication facts.

Basic Facts	$7 \times 9 = 63$	$3 \times 6 = 18$	$5 \times 8 = 40$
Extended Facts			

Unit 3

Name _____ Date _____

Problem-Solving Activity
Estimating Distances

Using the given object as the unit of measurement, estimate the distance between the set of points.

1. About how many skateboards is the distance from C to D?

2. About how many wheels is the distance from E to F?

3. About how many women is the distance from G to H?

mBook Reinforce Understanding
Use the mBook *Study Guide* to review lesson concepts.

Name _____ Date _____

 Skills Maintenance
Basic and Extended Multiplication Facts

Activity 1

Solve the set of basic and extended multiplication facts.

1. 7×8 _____
2. 9×3 _____
3. 4×6 _____

8×7 _____
3×9 _____
6×4 _____

7×80 _____
3×90 _____
6×40 _____

7×800 _____
3×900 _____
6×400 _____

Traditional Addition and Subtraction

Activity 2

Add or subtract.

1. $\begin{array}{r} 376 \\ + 129 \\ \hline \end{array}$

2. $\begin{array}{r} 204 \\ - 68 \\ \hline \end{array}$

3. $\begin{array}{r} 915 \\ - 792 \\ \hline \end{array}$

Name _____ Date _____

Apply Skills
Factoring Out a 10

Activity 1

Factor out a 10 from the numbers 40, 70, and 80.

Activity 2

Factor out a 10 from the numbers 700, 7,000, and 70,000.

Name _____ Date _____

 Problem-Solving Activity
More Estimating Distances

For each problem, look at the picture to determine an appropriate unit of measurement. Then estimate the distance between the labeled points.

1. Estimate the distance between points C and D.

C● ●D

2. Estimate the distance between points E and F.

E ● ●F

mBook Reinforce Understanding
Use the mBook *Study Guide* to review lesson concepts.

Name _____ Date _____

 Skills Maintenance
Basic and Extended Multiplication Facts

Activity 1

Solve the basic and extended facts.

1. 9 × 8 _____   2. 7 × 3 _____   3. 5 × 6 _____

   8 × 9 _____   3 × 7 _____   6 × 5 _____

   9 × 80 _____   3 × 70 _____   6 × 50 _____

   9 × 800 _____   3 × 700 _____   6 × 500 _____

Traditional Addition and Subtraction

Activity 2

Add or subtract.

1.　　488
　　+ 159

2.　　600
　　− 499

3.　　587
　　+ 294

Name _____ Date _____

% ÷ **Apply Skills**
= x
< x **Factoring Out Powers of 10**

Activity 1

Factor out all powers of 10 possible from the numbers below.

Number	? × Greatest Power of 10
5,000	5 × 1,000
300	
6,000	
700	
40	
8,000	

Activity 2

Factor out 10, 100, and 1,000 from each number.

Number	? × 10	? × 100	? × 1,000
70	7 × 10		
80			
400	40 × 10	4 × 100	
500			
900			
1,000	100 × 10	10 × 100	1 × 1,000
2,000			
3,000			
6,000			

Name _____ Date _____

 Problem-Solving Activity
Choosing a Unit of Measurement

Suppose the shoe of one of your classmates is selected as the official unit of measurement. Use your classmate's shoe as a measuring device and work in small groups to measure various lengths and distances in the classroom. Copy the chart below and fill in each distance you measure, making sure to correctly label your measurements. A model is provided below.

Distance	Measurement
From the teacher's desk to the door	8 shoes

mBook Reinforce Understanding
Use the mBook *Study Guide* to review lesson concepts.

Name _____ Date _____

Skills Maintenance
Basic and Extended Multiplication Facts

Activity 1

Solve the set of basic and extended multiplication facts.

1. 7×6 _____

   6×7 _____

   7×60 _____

   7×600 _____

2. 4×5 _____

   5×4 _____

   5×40 _____

   5×400 _____

3. 7×3 _____

   3×7 _____

   7×30 _____

   7×300 _____

Name _____ Date _____

 Apply Skills
Expanded Multiplication

Activity 1

Find the product using expanded multiplication.

Model	$\begin{array}{r} 95 \\ \times\ 3 \end{array}$	$\begin{array}{r} 90\ \vert\ \ \ 5 \\ \times\ \ \ \ \ \vert\ \ \ 3 \\ \hline 15 \\ +\ \ \ 270 \\ \hline 285 \end{array}$

1. $\begin{array}{r} 86 \\ \times\ 3 \end{array}$

2. $\begin{array}{r} 47 \\ \times\ 6 \end{array}$

3. $\begin{array}{r} 34 \\ \times\ 5 \end{array}$

4. $\begin{array}{r} 78 \\ \times\ 5 \end{array}$

Name _____ Date _____

Problem-Solving Activity
Making a Ruler

Let's create a ruler like the one below to use as a measuring device.

Use the strip of paper provided by your teacher to create a ruler. Then use your ruler to measure items in your classroom. Follow the steps.

Step 1: One ruler is one U.S. customary foot. There are 12 inches in one foot. Mark lines at both ends of your ruler. Label the left line **0** and the right line **12**.

Step 2: Fold the ruler in half. There are 12 inches on a ruler, so half of a ruler would be 6 inches. Open your ruler and make a line from top to bottom on the fold. Mark it **6**.

Step 3: Fold the ruler in half two more times. Label the fold halfway between the left side and the 6: **3**. Label the fold halfway between the 6 and the 12: **9**. Make the lines reach from top to bottom.

Step 4: Make two equally spaced markings between **0** and **3**, **3** and **6**, **6** and **9**, **9** and **12**. The marks should extend from top to bottom. Label them.

Step 5: Make a halfway mark between each of the inch markings. The lines should extend from the bottom and halfway to the top. Make sure the increments are equal in size. Label all of the half-inch lines $\frac{1}{2}$.

Step 6: Make the quarter-inch lines by marking halfway marks in the spaces between half inches and whole inches. For example, there should be a $\frac{1}{4}$ mark between the **zero** and the $\frac{1}{2}$. If you count the fourths in each whole inch, the first should be labeled $\frac{1}{2}$. The second fourth is $\frac{2}{4}$, or $\frac{1}{2}$. The third is $\frac{3}{4}$. The fourth is $\frac{4}{4}$, or a whole inch. The quarter-inch lines should extend from the bottom and they should be half as tall as the half-inch lines.

Step 7: Make halfway marks between each $\frac{1}{4}$ inch line. These are eighths. The lines should extend from the bottom and be about half as tall as the $\frac{1}{4}$ inch lines. Repeat between each $\frac{1}{8}$ inch line.

mBook Reinforce Understanding
Use the **mBook Study Guide** to review lesson concepts.

Name _____ Date _____

Skills Maintenance
Factoring Out Powers of 10

Activity 1

Complete the table using powers of 10, 100, and 1,000. An example is provided.

Number	? × 10	? × 100	? × 1,000
1,000	100 × 10	10 × 100	1 × 1,000
4,000			
5,000			
6,000			
8,000			
9,000			

Name _____ Date _____

Problem-Solving Activity
The Metric System

Use a metric ruler to measure the line segment in the specified unit.

1. A is _____ long.

A   _____

2. B is _____ long.

B   _____

3. C is _____ long.

C   _____

4. D is _____ long.

D

_____

5. E is _____ long.

E   _____

6. F is _____ long.

F   _____

7. G is _____ long.

G   _____

mBook **Reinforce Understanding**
Use the mBook *Study Guide* to review lesson concepts.

Name _____ Date _____

Skills Maintenance
Basic and Extended Multiplication Facts

Activity 1

Solve these basic and extended multiplication facts.

1. 3×7 _____

    3×70 _____

    3×700 _____

    $3 \times 7,000$ _____

2. 4×6 _____

    4×60 _____

    4×600 _____

    $4 \times 6,000$ _____

3. 5×5 _____

    5×50 _____

    5×500 _____

    $5 \times 5,000$ _____

4. 3×8 _____

    3×80 _____

    3×800 _____

    $3 \times 8,000$ _____

5. 2×1 _____

    2×10 _____

    2×100 _____

    $2 \times 1,000$ _____

6. 7×9 _____

    7×90 _____

    7×900 _____

    $7 \times 9,000$ _____

Name _____ Date _____

 Apply Skills
More Expanded Multiplication

Activity 1

Find the product using expanded multiplication.

1.　782
　×　3

2.　135
　×　2

3.　4,326
　×　4

4.　3,624
　×　4

Name _____ Date _____

Problem-Solving Activity
Estimating Metric Measurements

Estimate the length of each object. Think about the referents for the unit of measurement listed as the answer choice. Be sure to estimate the length of the object in real life, not the picture shown. Circle the best estimate and give a brief explanation for your answer choice.

1. About how long is a paper clip in real life?

    (a) 5 mm

    (b) 5 cm

    (c) 50 cm

    _____

    _____

2. About how long is a stapler in real life?

    (a) 10 m

    (b) 20 cm

    (c) 500 cm

    _____

    _____

3. About how long is a pencil in real life?

    (a) 15 mm

    (b) 15 cm

    (c) 15 m

    _____

    _____

mBook Reinforce Understanding
Use the mBook *Study Guide* to review lesson concepts.

Name _____ Date _____

 ## Skills Maintenance
Basic and Extended Multiplication Facts

Activity 1

Complete the basic and extended multiplication facts.

1. $4 \times \underline{\hspace{1.5cm}} = 20$ 2. $4 \times 50 = \underline{\hspace{1.5cm}}$ 3. $5 \times \underline{\hspace{1.5cm}} = 35$

4. $\underline{\hspace{1.5cm}} \times 4 = 24$ 5. $\underline{\hspace{1.5cm}} \times 6 = 24$ 6. $6 \times \underline{\hspace{1.5cm}} = 240$

7. $\underline{\hspace{1.5cm}} \times 9 = 81$ 8. $3 \times 90 = \underline{\hspace{1.5cm}}$ 9. $3 \times 900 = \underline{\hspace{1.5cm}}$

10. $7 \times \underline{\hspace{1.5cm}} = 56$ 11. $8 \times 7 = \underline{\hspace{1.5cm}}$ 12. $8 \times \underline{\hspace{1.5cm}} = 560$

Unit 3

Name _____ Date _____

 Apply Skills
Multiplying Two Multidigit Numbers

Activity 1

Find the products by using expanded multiplication.

1.   47
     × 28

     _____

2.   35
     × 74

     _____

3.   63
     × 79

     _____

Name _____ Date _____

 Problem-Solving Activity
Estimating Measurements

Picture each of the objects described in the problems. Estimate the length of the object. Think about the referents for the units of measurement listed as answer choices. Choose the best estimate for each problem. Write your answers below the problem. Be ready to explain the estimation strategy you used for each problem.

1. What is the approximate length of a brand new pencil?

    (a) 15 millimeters (mm)

    (b) 15 centimeters (cm)

    (c) 15 meters (m)

    _____

    _____

    _____

    _____

2. What is the approximate height of your desk?

    (a) 1 meter (m)

    (b) 1 centimeter (cm)

    (c) 1 millimeter (mm)

    _____

    _____

    _____

    _____

mBook **Reinforce Understanding**
Use the mBook *Study Guide* to review lesson concepts.

Name _____ Date _____

Skills Maintenance
Basic and Extended Multiplication Facts

Activity 1

Solve the basic and extended multiplication facts.

1. 8×7 _____

2. 8×6 _____

3. 6×5 _____

4. 2×9 _____

5. 8×70 _____

6. 600×8 _____

7. 50×60 _____

8. 20×9 _____

9. 80×600 _____

Name _____ Date _____

 Apply Skills
Which Method is More Efficient?

Activity 1

Find the product of 316 and 27 using traditional multiplication and expanded multiplication.

```
  316
×  27
```

_____

Activity 2

Look at the problems solved below using expanded and traditional multiplication. Compare the two methods. On a separate piece of paper, write at least two things that are the same about the methods and at least two things that are different.

Problem A:

```
   195            100 | 90 |   5          ³²
 ×   4          ×         |   4         195
                             20       ×   4
                            360        780
                        +   400
                            780
```

Problem B:

```
   27             20 |   7            27
 × 49           × 40 |   9          × 49
                        63           243
                       180        + 1,080
                       280          1,323
                 +     800
                     1,323
```

Name _____ Date _____

 ### Problem-Solving Activity
The World of Graphic Design

A graphic designer created this advertisement. She wants to measure certain elements of the design to check that the dimensions are correct. Use a metric ruler to measure the specified dimensions to the nearest centimeter.

Title of Advertisement

Words that Describe the Product

1. How wide is the box for the title? _____

2. How wide is the box for the description? _____

3. How tall is the box for the title? _____

4. How tall is the box for the description? _____

mBook Reinforce Understanding
Use the mBook *Study Guide* to review lesson concepts.

Name _____ Date _____

 Skills Maintenance
Multiplication Facts

Activity 1

Complete the extended multiplication facts.

1. $50 \times$ _____ $= 250$

2. $8 \times$ _____ $= 320$

3. $5 \times$ _____ $= 200$

4. $80 \times$ _____ $= 320$

5. $40 \times$ _____ $= 200$

6. $80 \times 40 =$ _____

7. $5 \times$ _____ $= 2,500$

8. $500 \times$ _____ $= 2,500$

9. $400 \times$ _____ $= 2,000$

Methods of Multiplication

Activity 2

Chose the best method for solving each problem: (a) estimation and a calculator, (b) mental math, or (c) traditional multiplication.

1. $\begin{array}{r} 32 \\ \times\ \ 3 \\ \hline \end{array}$

2. $\begin{array}{r} 468 \\ \times 527 \\ \hline \end{array}$

3. $\begin{array}{r} 600 \\ \times\ \ 40 \\ \hline \end{array}$

Name _____ Date _____

%÷ Apply Skills
=×
<× Estimating Products

Activity 1

Estimate the product by rounding to create an extended fact. Show your estimation on the number line. Then use a calculator to find the exact answer.

1.   29   29 rounds to _____.   _____   Estimate _____

   × 4   ×   4   Exact Answer _____

                                                    _____

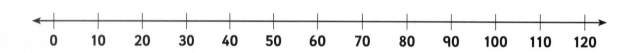

2.   792   792 rounds to _____.   _____   Estimate _____

   ×   3   ×   3   Exact Answer _____

                                                    _____

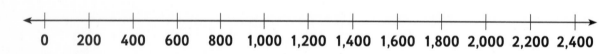

Activity 2

Estimate to solve the problem. Round the numbers in the word problems to create an extended fact. Write the extended fact you use.

1.   Tony has 3 pieces of board that are each 48 inches long. He is working on a project that calls for 28 boards that are each 6 inches long. Tony figures he can cut the boards he has into the smaller 6-inch boards he needs. Does he have enough board for the project?

   _____

   _____

   _____

Name _____ Date _____

 Problem-Solving Activity
Designing a Logo

As part of the design process, graphic designers sketch logos at various stages of their development to ensure the parts are the correct size. The sketch below shows a logo in the early stages of the design process. The graphic designer wants to make sure the triangles are the correct size before moving forward.

Recreate this sketch in the space below. Part of the logo has been started for you. Measure the sides of the triangles to make sure you draw them correctly.

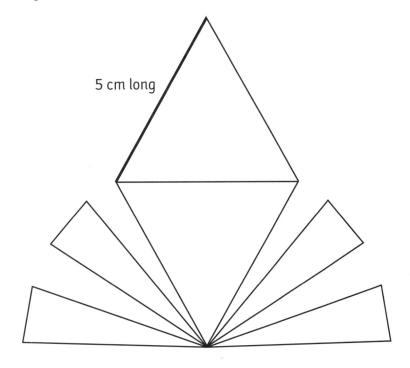

5 cm long

mBook **Reinforce Understanding**
Use the mBook *Study Guide* to review lesson concepts.

Name _____ Date _____

Skills Maintenance
Traditional Multiplication

Activity 1

Use traditional multiplication to find the product.

1.
$$\begin{array}{r} 638 \\ \times\ \ \ 4 \\ \hline \end{array}$$

2.
$$\begin{array}{r} 92 \\ \times 15 \\ \hline \end{array}$$

3.
$$\begin{array}{r} 67 \\ \times 64 \\ \hline \end{array}$$

Name _____ Date _____

 Apply Skills
Common Errors in Multiplication

Activity 1

Some of the problems contain an error. Find and describe each error, then solve the problem correctly.

1. $\overset{3}{3}9$
    $\times\ 7$
    $\overline{246}$

2. $\overset{2}{2}31$
    $\times\ \ 9$
    $\overline{2{,}079}$

3. $\overset{5}{8}9$
    $\times\ 6$
    $\overline{484}$

_____

_____

_____

_____

_____

_____

mBook Reinforce Understanding
Use the mBook *Study Guide* to review lesson concepts.

Name _____ Date _____

 Skills Maintenance
Extended Multiplication Facts

Activity 1

Complete the extended multiplication facts.

1. $70 = 7 \times$ _____   2. $700 = 70 \times$ _____   3. $400 = 4 \times$ _____

4. $600 = 6 \times$ _____   5. $800 = 80 \times$ _____   6. $400 = 40 \times$ _____

7. $400 =$ _____ $\times 10$ 8. $70 = 7 \times$ _____   9. $20 =$ _____ $\times 10$

Methods of Multiplication

Activity 2

Choose the best method for solving the problem: (a) estimation and a calculator, (b) mental math, or (c) traditional multiplication.

1. $\begin{array}{r} 42 \\ \times\ 3 \\ \hline \end{array}$ 2. $\begin{array}{r} 679 \\ \times\ 48 \\ \hline \end{array}$ 3. $\begin{array}{r} 90 \\ \times 40 \\ \hline \end{array}$

Name _____ Date _____

 Apply Skills
More Estimation of Products

Activity 1

Use estimation to find the approximate answer to the problems. Check your answer with a calculator.

1.   79
    × 43   _____ × _____ = _____

    Estimate _____

    Calculator Answer _____

    Is the calculator answer reasonable? _____

2.   48
    × 24   _____ × _____ = _____

    Estimate _____

    Calculator Answer _____

    Is the calculator answer reasonable? _____

3.   21
    × 89   _____ × _____ = _____

    Estimate _____

    Calculator Answer _____

    Is the calculator answer reasonable? _____

Name _____ Date _____

 ## Problem-Solving Activity
Designing a Web Page

The main part of the web page will show six different styles of hats sold by The Hat Factory. Customers can click on the pictures to shop for various hats of that style. Using the worksheet provided, position the pictures on the main part of the page in a way that is attractive and symmetrical.

1. Draw a square for each type of hat. You do not need to draw pictures of the hats. Instead label each square with the type of hat it represents.

2. Each side of the square should be 2 centimeters long.

3. Write the name of the company in the space at the top of the web page.

mBook Reinforce Understanding
Use the mBook *Study Guide* to review lesson concepts.

Name _____ Date _____

 ## Skills Maintenance
Basic and Extended Multiplication Facts

Activity 1

Solve the basic or extended multiplication fact.

1. 6×9 _____

2. 5×7 _____

3. 4×8 _____

4. 6×90 _____

5. 5×70 _____

6. 4×80 _____

7. 6×900 _____

8. 5×700 _____

9. 4×800 _____

Traditional Multiplication

Activity 2

Use traditional multiplication to find the product.

1.
$$\begin{array}{r} 36 \\ \times\ 5 \\ \hline \end{array}$$

2.
$$\begin{array}{r} 387 \\ \times\ 6 \\ \hline \end{array}$$

3.
$$\begin{array}{r} 42 \\ \times 37 \\ \hline \end{array}$$

Name _____ Date _____

Problem-Solving Activity
Measuring to Design a Company Logo

Four Triangle Productions, a company that produces movies, has hired a designer to create a new logo. They want it to consist of two small triangles, one medium triangle, and one large triangle. After the layout is complete, the designer will add color and other effects to the logo. The chart shows the dimensions for each triangle.

Triangle	Length of Two Sides
Small	2 cm
Medium	4 cm
Large	6 cm

Follow these steps to create a logo for Four Triangle Productions on the worksheet provided.

1. Use the picture below as a guide for the placement of the triangles.

2. Use the chart above to correctly measure and draw each triangle. The lengths of two sides of the triangle are specified. Draw the third side by connecting the other two sides of the triangle.

3. Include the name of the company in the logo.

mBook Reinforce Understanding
Use the mBook *Study Guide* to review lesson concepts.

Name _____ Date _____

Skills Maintenance
Extended Multiplication Facts

Activity 1

Solve the extended multiplication facts.

1. 60×40 _____
2. 100×10 _____
3. 900×10 _____

4. 6×400 _____
5. 100×100 _____
6. 50×70 _____

7. 90×10 _____
8. 70×5 _____
9. 90×60 _____

Traditional Multiplication

Activity 2

Use traditional multiplication to find the product.

1. $\begin{array}{r} 865 \\ \times\ \ \ 4 \\ \hline \end{array}$

2. $\begin{array}{r} 728 \\ \times\ \ \ 5 \\ \hline \end{array}$

3. $\begin{array}{r} 79 \\ \times 89 \\ \hline \end{array}$

Name _____ Date _____

Apply Skills
More Estimation with Multidigit Factors

Activity 1

Use estimation and a calculator to find the products.

1. 2,035
    × 323   _____ × _____ = _____

    Estimate _____   Calculator Answer _____

2. 581
    × 743   _____ × _____ = _____

    Estimate _____   Calculator Answer _____

3. 7,333
    ×   17   _____ × _____ = _____

    Estimate _____   Calculator Answer _____

4. 488
    × 132   _____ × _____ = _____

    Estimate _____   Calculator Answer _____

5. 1,342
    ×   58   _____ × _____ = _____

    Estimate _____   Calculator Answer _____

Name _____ Date _____

Problem-Solving Activity
Scale Drawings

Look at the scale drawing which shows the blueprint for the first floor of a new house. Each room is a different size than it will be in real life, but looks the right size in relation to the other rooms in the drawing.

Use a metric ruler to measure the dimensions of each room in centimeters. Write your answers in each room.

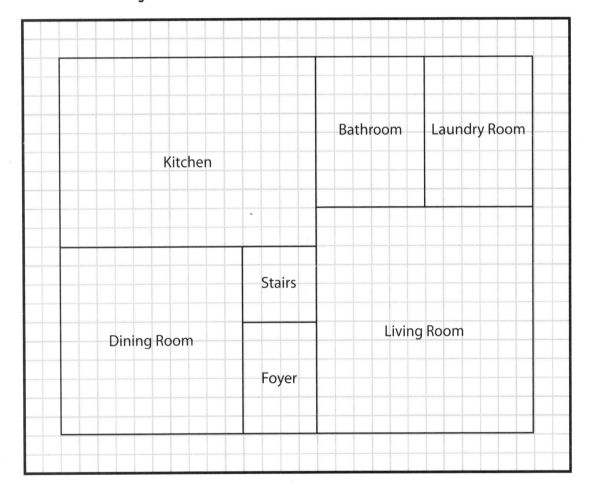

mBook Reinforce Understanding
Use the mBook *Study Guide* to review lesson concepts.

Unit 3 • Lesson 13   **129**

Name _____ Date _____

 Skills Maintenance
Methods of Multiplication

Activity 1

Choose the best method for solving the problem: (a) estimation and a calculator, (b) mental math, or (c) traditional multiplication.

1.   40
    × 30

2.   679
    × 43

3.   21
    ×   2

4.   213
    ×   3

5.   600
    × 900

6.   876
    × 429

Name _____ Date _____

 Problem-Solving Activity
Comparing Amounts in a Bar Graph

Axis Software Company is having a hard time selling its software. The bar graph shows their sales for the last six months. Use the bar graph to answer the questions.

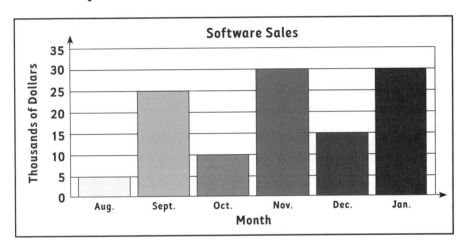

1. What were the total sales for the six months shown in the graph?

   _____

   _____

2. How much more were sales in November than in September?

   _____

3. How many times as great were sales in September than August?

   _____

4. Write a sentence using the phrase *times as great* to compare the sales in October with the sales in November.

   _____

   _____

 **Reinforce Understanding**
Use the mBook *Study Guide* to review lesson concepts.

Name _____ Date _____

 Skills Maintenance
Multiplication Facts

Activity 1

Complete the turn-around multiplication facts.

1. $7 \times 8 = 8 \times$ _____ $= 56$

2. $5 \times 6 = 6 \times 5 =$ _____

3. $9 \times$ _____ $= 6 \times 9 = 54$

4. $4 \times 8 = 8 \times$ _____ $=$ _____

Activity 2

Complete the basic and extended multiplication facts.

1. 7×9 _____

2. 6×8 _____

3. 7×90 _____

4. 6×80 _____

5. 7×900 _____

6. 6×800 _____

Name _____ Date _____

Unit Review
Multiplication

Activity 1

Complete the table.

Starting Number	? × 10
50	5 × 10
60	
70	
80	
90	

Activity 2

Use extended multiplication to find the product.

1.
```
    37
  ×  4
```

2.
```
    98
  ×  6
```

Activity 3

Complete the table by writing the number as a factor of 10, 100, and 1,000.

Starting Number	? × 10	? × 100	? × 1,000
7,000			
8,000			

Name _____ Date _____

Activity 4

Find the products using traditional multiplication.

1.	48	**2.**	54	**3.**	96	**4.**	87
	× 5		× 8		× 7		× 9

Activity 5

Estimate the answers by rounding the numbers and finding the extended multiplication facts.

1.   27
       × 4   Estimated Extended Fact _____

2.   61
       × 37   Estimated Extended Fact _____

3.   419
       × 78   Estimated Extended Fact _____

Activity 6

The problem contains an error. Use estimation and a calculator to find the correct answer. Then write a sentence describing the error.

1.   79
       × 3   Estimation _____

                  Calculator Answer _____

                  _____

                  _____

                  _____

Name _____ Date _____

Unit Review
Measurement

Activity 1

Estimate the correct unit of measurement using what you know about referents. Explain the reason for your answer.

1. About how long is a baseball bat in real life? *(not this drawing)*

   (a) 10 millimeters

   (b) 1 centimeter

   (c) 1 meter

   Why? _____

   _____

2. About how long are the skis in real life? *(not this drawing)*

   (a) 2 meters

   (b) 12 meters

   (c) 20 meters

   Why? _____

   _____

3. About how long is the ship in real life? *(not this drawing)*

   (a) 10 meters

   (b) 100 meters

   (c) 100 centimeters

   Why? _____

   _____

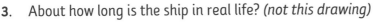

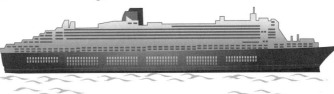

Unit 3

mBook Reinforce Understanding
Use the mBook *Study Guide* to review lesson concepts.

This page intentionally left blank.

Name _____ Date _____

 Skills Maintenance
Basic Multiplication Facts

Activity 1

Solve the basic facts.

1. 7×6 _____

2. 7×8 _____

3. 5×7 _____

4. 9×3 _____

5. 6×3 _____

6. 6×7 _____

7. 8×9 _____

8. 3×9 _____

Name _____ Date _____

%÷=<x Apply Skills
Multiplication and Division Fact Families

Activity 1

Write fact families for each group of numbers.

Model	**9, 8, and 72**
	$9 \times 8 = 72$
	$8 \times 9 = 72$
	$72 \div 9 = 8$
	$72 \div 8 = 9$

1. 6, 7, and 42   **2.** 5, 7, and 35   **3.** 8, 7, and 56

4. 8, 9, and 72   **5.** 3, 9, and 27   **6.** 3, 6, and 18

Activity 2

Complete the division facts.

1. $40 \div 5$ _____   **2.** $15 \div 3$ _____

3. $14 \div 7$ _____   **4.** $63 \div 9$ _____

5. $36 \div 6$ _____   **6.** $32 \div 8$ _____

Name _____ Date _____

Problem-Solving Activity
Measuring Square Units

Estimate the number of square units inside the shape. Write a sentence or two explaining how you got your answer.

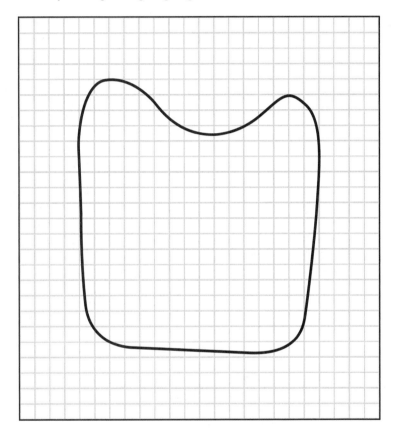

Explain how you got your answer.

_____

_____

_____

mBook Reinforce Understanding
Use the mBook *Study Guide* to review lesson concepts.

Name _____ Date _____

 Skills Maintenance
Fact Families

Activity 1

Write the fact family for each set of numbers.

1. 6, 4, and 24

2. 8, 6, and 48

3. 5, 9, and 45

Name _____ Date _____

%÷ Apply Skills
<×x Basic and Extended Division Facts

Activity 1

Write three extended facts for the basic facts.

1. $6 \div 2 = 3$ **2.** $56 \div 7 = 8$ **3.** $42 \div 6 = 7$

Activity 2

Use facts to complete the table.

Basic Fact	10s Fact	100s Fact
$54 \div 6 = 9$	$540 \div 6 = 90$	$5,400 \div 6 = 900$
$81 \div 9 = 9$		$8,100 \div 9 = 900$
$36 \div 4 = 9$	$360 \div 4 = 90$	
		$2,400 \div 4 = 600$
$72 \div 8 = 9$		$7,200 \div 8 = 900$
	$120 \div 4 = 30$	

Activity 3

Solve the basic and extended division facts.

1. $9\overline{)27}$ **2.** $7\overline{)42}$ **3.** $3\overline{)240}$ **4.** $9\overline{)270}$

Unit 4

Name _____ Date _____

 Problem-Solving Activity
Comparing Sizes of Shapes

Which of these shapes is the largest? Tell how you got your answer.

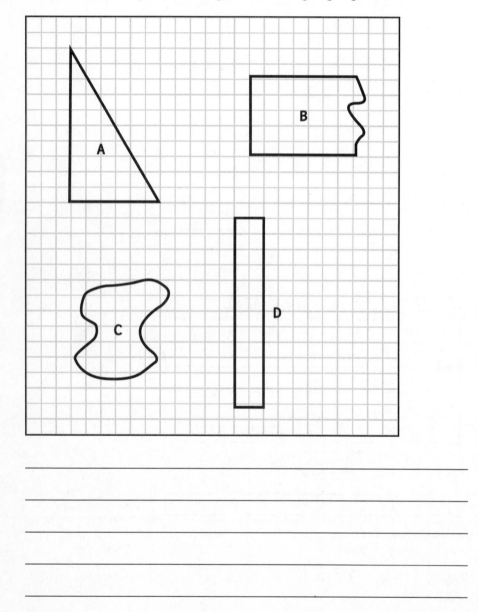

_____

_____

_____

_____

_____

_____

mBook Reinforce Understanding
Use the mBook *Study Guide* to review lesson concepts.

Name _____ Date _____

Skills Maintenance
Basic and Extended Division Facts

Activity 1

Solve the basic and extended division facts.

1. $9\overline{)18}$ 2. $5\overline{)450}$ 3. $7\overline{)490}$ 4. $8\overline{)64}$

Activity 2

Complete the basic and extended division facts.

1. $18 \div \underline{\hspace{1.5cm}} = 2$

2. $490 \div \underline{\hspace{1.5cm}} = 70$

3. $450 \div 9 = \underline{\hspace{1.5cm}}$

4. $\underline{\hspace{1.5cm}} \div 8 = 8$

Unit 4

Name _____ Date _____

Apply Skills
Basic Division Facts on a Number Line

Activity 1

Solve the division problem. Then show how the problem is broken into units on a number line.

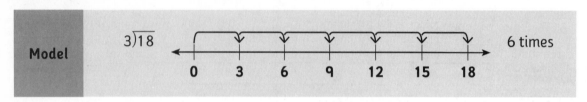

| Model | $3\overline{)18}$ ... 6 times |

1. Show this problem on the number line: $7\overline{)21}$

2. Show this problem on the number line: $6\overline{)24}$

3. Show this problem on the number line: $7\overline{)28}$

Activity 2

Write out the problem demonstrated on the number lines.

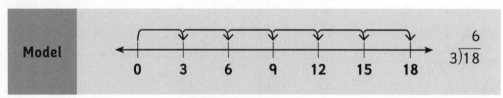

| Model | $3\overline{)18}$ with quotient 6 |

1. The problem shown is _____.

2. The problem shown is _____.

Name _____ Date _____

 ## Problem-Solving Activity
Same Shape, Different Size

Find the area of Object A and Object B. Remember to answer using square units by counting the square units for each object.

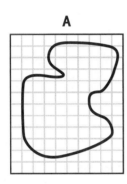

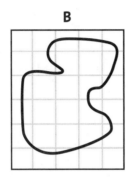

Area of Object A _____

Area of Object B _____

Tell why the measurements for the two objects are different.

_____

_____

_____

mBook Reinforce Understanding
Use the mBook *Study Guide* to review lesson concepts.

Name _____ Date _____

 Skills Maintenance
Number Lines

Activity 1

Write out the problem demonstrated on the number lines.

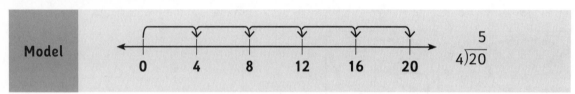

1. The problem shown is _____.

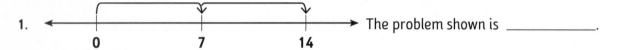

2. The problem shown is _____.

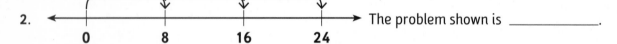

3. The problem shown is _____.

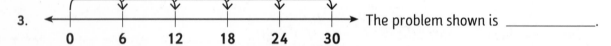

4. The problem shown is _____.

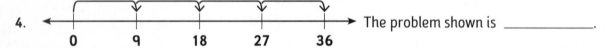

Multiplication

Activity 2

Tell whether you would solve the problem using (a) traditional multiplication, (b) estimation and a calculator, or (c) mental math. Do not solve.

1.
$$200 \\ \times\ 40$$
Method _____

2.
$$367 \\ \times 487$$
Method _____

3.
$$421 \\ \times\ \ 2$$
Method _____

Name _____ Date _____

%÷ Apply Skills
Extended Division Facts on a Number Line

Activity 1

Show the extended division facts on a number line.

1.
$$6\overline{)120} = 20$$

← ———————————————————————— →

2.
$$3\overline{)60} = 20$$

← ———————————————————————— →

Activity 2

Write out the problem demonstrated on the number lines.

1. The problem shown is _____.

0 3 6 9 12 15 18 21 24 27 30 33 36 39 42 45 48 51 54 57 60

2. The problem shown is _____.

0   9   18   27   36

Activity 3

Use mental math to fill in the missing extended division facts.

Basic Fact	10s Fact	100s Fact
72 ÷ 8 = 9	720 ÷ 8 = 90	7,200 ÷ 8 = 900
49 ÷ 7 = 7		4,900 ÷ 7 = 700
		2,500 ÷ 5 = 500
	240 ÷ 6 = 40	
42 ÷ 7 = 6		
		2,700 ÷ 9 = 300
		1,600 ÷ 4 = 400

Name _____ Date _____

 ## Problem-Solving Activity
Finding Area by Counting Squares

Answer the questions about the star-shaped design. Here's a hint: You don't have to count every square to figure out the size of each object. Give your answers in square units. For each question, round your answer to the nearest 10.

1. About how big is the small star in the center?

    _____

2. About how big is the larger star?

    _____

3. About how much larger is the larger star than the smaller star? (Be sure to include the size of the smaller star inside of the larger star when you figure this out.)

    _____

4. About how big is the whole space inside the circle?

    _____

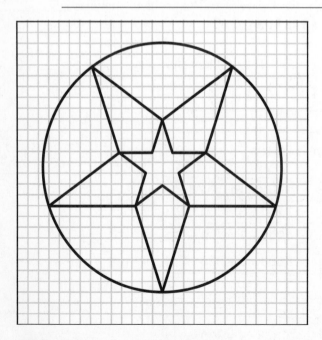

mBook Reinforce Understanding
Use the mBook *Study Guide* to review lesson concepts.

Name _____ Date _____

 Skills Maintenance
Basic and Extended Division Facts

Activity 1

Solve the basic and extended division facts.

1. $6\overline{)18}$ 2. $9\overline{)450}$ 3. $4\overline{)24}$ 4. $6\overline{)360}$

Finding Area

Activity 2

Find the size of the rectangle by counting the square units.

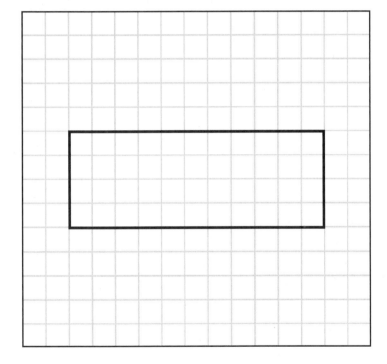

Area of the rectangle _____

Unit 4

Name _____ Date _____

Apply Skills
Remainders

Activity 1

Solve the problems using long division.

1. $6\overline{)58}$

2. $7\overline{)38}$

Activity 2

Solve the problems using your calculator. Then answer the questions.

1. $4\overline{)34}$ How many equal units of 4 are in 34? _____

    What's the decimal number remainder? _____

2. $8\overline{)52}$ How many equal units of 8 are in 52? _____

    What's the decimal number remainder? _____

Activity 3

Use what you know about division facts and remainders to solve the problems. Then show the problem on the number line. Circle the remainder as shown in the model.

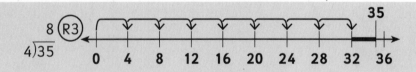

Model	8 (R3) $4\overline{)35}$

1. $3\overline{)23}$ ⟵——————————————⟶

2. $6\overline{)41}$ ⟵——————————————⟶

mBook Reinforce Understanding
Use the mBook *Study Guide* to review lesson concepts.

Name _____ Date _____

Skills Maintenance
Basic and Extended Division Facts

Activity 1

Complete the basic and extended division facts.

1. $32 \div 8 =$ _____

2. $36 \div$ _____ $= 9$

3. $42 \div$ _____ $= 7$

4. _____ $\div 9 = 80$

5. $270 \div 3 =$ _____

6. $240 \div$ _____ $= 60$

Name _____ Date _____

Apply Skills
Rounding Strategies in Division

Activity 1

Solve the division problems. Round each answer to the nearest whole number.

1. $34 \div 8$

   Rounded Answer _____

2. $58 \div 7$

   Rounded Answer _____

3. $27 \div 4$

   Rounded Answer _____

4. $17 \div 2$

   Rounded Answer _____

Name _____ Date _____

 Problem-Solving Activity
Estimating Square Units on a Map

Below is a map of the city of San Francisco, California. San Francisco is one of the most crowded cities in the United States. Each full square contains about 26,400 people. Note that not all squares are full squares, so you are going to have to combine partial squares to make full squares.

Answer the questions about the map.

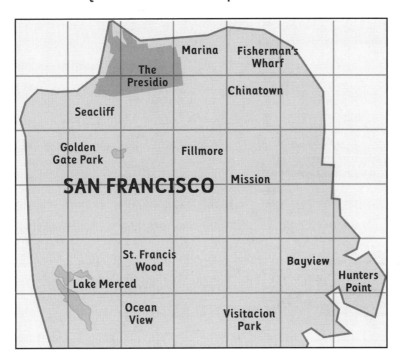

1. The Presidio is shaded on the map. What is its approximate population?

   _____

2. Explain how you got your answer.

   _____

   _____

   _____

mBook Reinforce Understanding
Use the mBook *Study Guide* to review lesson concepts.

Name _____ Date _____

Skills Maintenance
Division With a Calculator

Activity 1

Look at the calculator display for each problem. Then round the answer to the nearest whole number.

1. 6)‾13‾

    Calculator Answer 2.166667

    Rounded Answer _____

2. 9)‾85‾

    Calculator Answer 9.444444

    Rounded Answer _____

3. 8)‾50‾

    Calculator Answer 6.25

    Rounded Answer _____

4. 3)‾19‾

    Calculator Answer 6.333333

    Rounded Answer _____

Name _____ Date _____

Apply Skills
Near Fact Division

Activity 1

Estimate the answers to the problems by rounding to the nearest fact. Then solve the original problem with a calculator to see how close your estimation was.

Model	$8\overline{)57}$ Near Fact $\dfrac{7}{8\overline{)56}}$ Calculator Answer ___7.125___

1. $6\overline{)13}$

    Near Fact _____

    Calculator Answer _____

2. $9\overline{)85}$

    Near Fact _____

    Calculator Answer _____

3. $7\overline{)44}$

    Near Fact _____

    Calculator Answer _____

4. $8\overline{)34}$

    Near Fact _____

    Calculator Answer _____

5. $4\overline{)31}$

    Near Fact _____

    Calculator Answer _____

6. $5\overline{)34}$

    Near Fact _____

    Calculator Answer _____

7. $2\overline{)19}$

    Near Fact _____

    Calculator Answer _____

8. $9\overline{)73}$

    Near Fact _____

    Calculator Answer _____

Name _____ Date _____

 ## Problem-Solving Activity
Using Division in Everyday Life

The four members of the Scatter Plots are deciding how to split the money they made over the past month. The table shows how much money the group made for its last six concerts. Use your calculator to answer the questions.

The Scatter Plots' May Concert Tour in California		
Date	**Concert**	**Profit**
May 1	San Diego	$2,400
May 2	Anaheim	$1,440
May 8	Long Beach	$4,260
May 9	Riverside	$3,700
May 15	Los Angeles	$6,020
May 16	Santa Barbara	$4,040

1. How much should each person in the group get if the money from all of the concerts was divided equally among the group members?

   _____

2. Altogether, about 4,200 people attended the six concerts. If about the same number of people attended each concert, what was the approximate attendance at each concert?

   _____

3. At which concert did each band member make the most money?

   _____

mBook Reinforce Understanding
Use the mBook *Study Guide* to review lesson concepts.

Name _____ Date _____

Skills Maintenance
Estimating Near Facts

Activity 1

Estimate the answer by finding a near fact.

Model	$6\overline{)38}$	$\overset{6}{6\overline{)36}}$	Estimate <u>6</u>

1. $3\overline{)29}$

   Near fact _____

   Estimate _____

2. $8\overline{)37}$

   Near fact _____

   Estimate _____

3. $7\overline{)55}$

   Near fact _____

   Estimate _____

4. $9\overline{)84}$

   Near fact _____

   Estimate _____

Name _____ Date _____

Apply Skills
Place Value and Long Division

Activity 1

Solve the long division problems. As you work each step on the right, fill in the place-value table on the left.

1. Place Value $2\overline{)486}$ Long Division $2\overline{)486}$

Hundreds	Tens	Ones

2. Place Value $3\overline{)99}$ Long Division $3\overline{)99}$

Hundreds	Tens	Ones

3. Place Value $4\overline{)848}$ Long Division $4\overline{)848}$

Hundreds	Tens	Ones

4. Place Value $2\overline{)666}$ Long Division $2\overline{)666}$

Hundreds	Tens	Ones

Name _____ Date _____

 Problem-Solving Activity
Division in Word Problems

Solve the word problems. If there is a remainder, decide what to do with it. Be ready to explain your thoughts.

1. Tatiana's teacher received 45 free tickets to a local amusement park. Tatiana and five other students were selected to receive the tickets. If the tickets are divided evenly among the students, how many tickets will each one receive?

    _____

    _____

    _____

    _____

    _____

2. Sebastian and two friends pooled their money and bought eight packages of baseball cards. There were six cards in each package. They decided to divide the cards out evenly. How many cards will each person get?

    _____

3. Tim plays in a band with four other friends. They just got their first gig at a local coffee shop. The owner said he would pay them $50 for the gig. If they divide the money evenly, how much will each person get?

    _____

4. Michael and his grandmother went to a play with eight other people. They needed taxi rides back home after the play. Michael called and found out each taxi can hold four people besides the driver. How many taxis will they need?

    _____

    _____

mBook Reinforce Understanding
Use the mBook *Study Guide* to review lesson concepts.

Name _____ Date _____

 Skills Maintenance
Basic Division

Activity 1

Solve the problems and fill in the place-value table.

1. 2)226   Long Division   2)226

Hundreds	Tens	Ones

2. 4)488   Long Division   4)488

Hundreds	Tens	Ones

3. 3)639   Long Division   3)639

Hundreds	Tens	Ones

Name _____ Date _____

 Apply Skills
Regrouping in Division

Activity 1

Complete the problems using a place-value table. As you work each step on the right, fill in the place-value table on the left.

1. Place Value   2)146   Long Division   2)146

Hundreds	Tens	Ones

2. Place Value   3)129   Long Division   3)129

Hundreds	Tens	Ones

3. Place Value   4)244   Long Division   4)244

Hundreds	Tens	Ones

Name _____ Date _____

Problem-Solving Activity
Making Division Word Problems

Write two division word problems. Each problem should have at least three sentences. Be creative. Your problems can include only words or they can also involve a drawing, a graph, or a table of numbers. Be sure to answer your problems and show your work. Be prepared to explain how your problems involve division.

_____

_____

_____

_____

_____

_____

_____

_____

_____

mBook Reinforce Understanding
Use the mBook *Study Guide* to review lesson concepts.

Name _____ Date _____

Skills Maintenance
Estimating Area

Activity 1

Look at the star design. Count the square units in the star. About how big is the design?

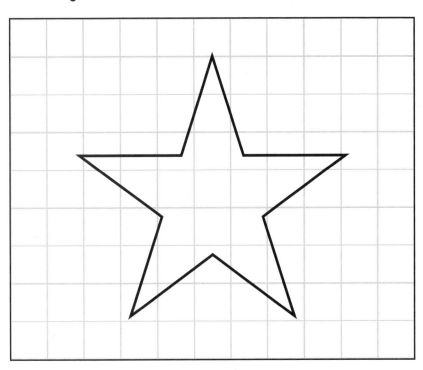

Name _____ Date _____

 Apply Skills
Traditional Long Division

Activity 1

Complete the problems using traditional long division. Check your answers.

1. $2\overline{)116}$

2. $3\overline{)228}$

3. $4\overline{)372}$

4. $5\overline{)245}$

mBook Reinforce Understanding
Use the mBook *Study Guide* to review lesson concepts.

Name _____ Date _____

Skills Maintenance
Long Division

Activity 1

Solve the problems using long division.

1. $7\overline{)413}$

2. $8\overline{)592}$

3. $9\overline{)837}$

4. $6\overline{)294}$

Name _____ Date _____

%÷=<x Apply Skills
Using Near Extended Facts to Estimate

Activity 1

Rewrite the problems using near extended facts. Do not solve the original problems.

Model	$8\overline{)562}$
	$\overset{70}{8\overline{)560}}$
	Near Extended Fact $8\overline{)560}$

1. $6\overline{)122}$

   Near Extended Fact _____

2. $9\overline{)178}$

   Near Extended Fact _____

3. $4\overline{)203}$

   Near Extended Fact _____

4. $5\overline{)356}$

   Near Extended Fact _____

5. $7\overline{)488}$

   Near Extended Fact _____

Name _____ Date _____

 Problem-Solving Activity
Measurement in Architecture

Answer the questions based on the blueprint drawing. Hint: When you figure out how many square units a room is, don't worry about the doors on the inside of the room. Similarly, when you figure out the size of the inside of the house, don't worry about the doors, inside walls, or windows.

1. How big is the inside of the house, including all of the rooms?

   _____

2. Draw lines so that each room is a rectangle. This will be especially important for the kitchen and the living room.

   Which room is the biggest?

   _____

   Which room is the smallest?

   _____

   How much bigger is the kitchen than the bathroom?

   _____

   How much bigger is bedroom B than bedroom A?

   _____

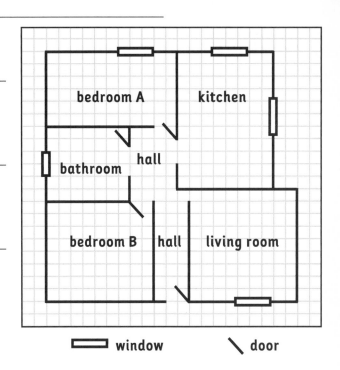

mBook Reinforce Understanding
Use the mBook *Study Guide* to review lesson concepts.

Name _____ Date _____

Skills Maintenance
Multiplication and Division

Activity 1

Rewrite the problems as near extended facts. Do not solve the original problems.

1. $7\overline{)489}$

    Near Fact _____

2. $6\overline{)419}$

    Near Fact _____

Activity 2

Tell whether you would solve the problem using (a) traditional multiplication, (b) estimation and a calculator, or (c) mental math. Do not solve.

1. $\begin{array}{r} 600 \\ \times\ \ \ 3 \end{array}$ Best Method _____

2. $\begin{array}{r} 437 \\ \times 987 \end{array}$ Best Method _____

3. $\begin{array}{r} 123 \\ \times\ \ \ 3 \end{array}$ Best Method _____

Name _____ Date _____

Apply Skills
Estimating in Division

Activity 1

Rewrite both numbers to make a near extended fact. Pull out the 10s.
Solve the basic fact.

Model	$91\overline{)371}$ Near Extended Fact $\dfrac{4}{90\overline{)360}}$
	$9 \times 10\overline{)36 \times 10} \rightarrow 9\overline{)36}^{\,4}$

1. $21\overline{)63}$

    Near Extended Fact _____

2. $32\overline{)89}$

    Near Extended Fact _____

3. $49\overline{)279}$

    Near Extended Fact _____

4. $38\overline{)406}$

    Near Extended Fact _____

Unit 4

Name _____ Date _____

Problem-Solving Activity
Designing Your Own Floor Plan

Here's a chance to design your own living room. Put at least four objects in the room. They could be chairs, couches, a TV, shelves, a coffee table, or anything else that might go in the living room.

Before you draw the objects, think about how big they should be, and write the information in the table. Then draw the objects on the floor plan. Be sure to label the objects.

Name of the Object	Number of Square Units

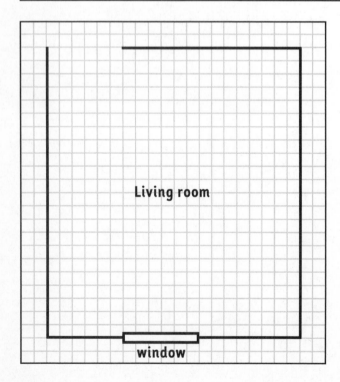

Living room

window

mBook Reinforce Understanding
Use the mBook *Study Guide* to review lesson concepts.

Name _____ Date _____

Skills Maintenance
Traditional Division Problems

Activity 1

Solve the problems using long division.

1. 8⟌49

2. 7⟌65

3. 9⟌378

4. 6⟌444

Name _____ Date _____

%÷ Apply Skills
Finding Division Errors

Activity 1

A student used a calculator to solve the problems. She got the wrong answers. Use your skills to find a near fact for each problem, find the exact answer on a calculator, then describe the error that the student made.

Problem 1: $7\overline{)31}$

She got this answer on her calculator:

0.22580645161209

1. Estimate the answer by finding a near fact. _____

2. Find the exact answer on a calculator. _____

3. Describe the error the student made.

_____

_____

Problem 2: $8\overline{)91}$

She got this answer on her calculator:

2.375

1. Estimate the answer by finding a near fact. _____

2. Find the exact answer on a calculator. _____

3. Describe the error the student made.

_____

_____

Name _____ Date _____

 Problem-Solving Activity
Building Design

Estimate the answers to the problems.

1. A skyscraper is 89 stories tall. Every tenth floor must have special beams to support the building. About how many floors need special beams?

   _____

2. If you look at the drawing, there are two columns of windows on each side of the building. Each column contains 1 large window at each floor. About how many windows are there on one side of the 89-story building?

   _____

3. The architecture company Korslund and Associates is leasing the entire 35th floor of the building. There are six large rooms on that floor. The company will use five of the rooms for its architects. It will put 20 drawing tables in each of these five rooms. How many drawing tables does the company need?

   _____

mBook **Reinforce Understanding**
Use the mBook *Study Guide* to review lesson concepts.

Unit 4

Name _____ Date _____

 Skills Maintenance
Long Division

Activity 1

Solve the problems using long division.

1. 9)67

2. 4)38

3. 8)616

4. 3)231

Name _____ Date _____

Apply Skills
More Division Errors

Activity 1

A student used a calculator to solve the problems. She got the wrong answers. Use your skills to find a near fact for each problem, find the exact answer on a calculator, then describe the error that the student made.

Problem 1: 21)192

Here is the answer the student got.

6.1428514285

1. Estimate the answer by finding a near fact. _____

2. Find the exact answer on a calculator. _____

3. Describe the error the student made.

    _____

    _____

Problem 2: 78)656

Here is the answer the student got.

0.118902439

1. Estimate the answer by finding a near fact. _____

2. Find the exact answer on a calculator. _____

3. Describe the error the student made.

    _____

    _____

Name _____ Date _____

 ## Problem-Solving Activity
Square Units and Triangular Units

The design is going to be used on the floor at the entrance to the Arena Building. Some of the shapes in the design are the same. You can figure out the size of the different shapes by counting the number of square units. But you can figure out its size more closely by counting the number of triangular units.

Think carefully about how you will answer the questions. You can find the answers to these questions without counting the units every time.

1. What is the total number of square units in both large triangles? What is the total number of triangular units in both large triangles?

_____

2. What is the total numbers of square units in both small triangles? What is the total number of triangular units in both small triangles?

_____

3. What is the total number of square units in the rectangle shapes? What is the total number of triangular units in the rectangle shapes?

_____

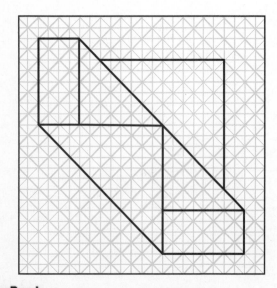

 mBook Reinforce Understanding
Use the mBook *Study Guide* to review lesson concepts.

Name _____ Date _____

Skills Maintenance
Basic Division Facts

Activity 1

Complete the basic division facts by finding the missing number.

1. $42 \div x = 6$ _____

2. $x \div 8 = 8$ _____

3. $72 \div 9 = x$ _____

4. $27 \div 9 = x$ _____

5. $35 \div x = 7$ _____

6. $45 \div x = 5$ _____

Name _____ Date _____

 Unit Review
Division

Activity 1

Solve the basic and extended facts.

1. 56 ÷ 8 _____ 560 ÷ 8 _____ 5,600 ÷ 8 _____

2. 49 ÷ 7 _____ 490 ÷ 7 _____ 4,900 ÷ 7 _____

Activity 2

Write fact families. Fill in the missing values for **X, Y, and Z**.

1. X, 7, and 63 **2.** 6, 8, and Y **3.** 5, Z, and 35

Activity 3

Estimate the answers by finding the closest basic fact.

1. 6)‾43 Near Fact _____

2. 7)‾50 Near Fact _____

Activity 4

Estimate the answers by finding the closest extended fact.

1. 31)‾249 Near Extended Fact _____

2. 39)‾281 Near Extended Fact _____

Name _____ Date _____

Activity 5

Solve the problems using traditional long division.

1. $6\overline{)372}$ 2. $7\overline{)504}$ 3. $8\overline{)592}$

Activity 6

Fill in the missing items in the table. Rewrite the near extended facts by pulling out the 10s. Then rewrite the problem as a basic fact and solve.

Near Extended Fact	Pull Out the 10s	Basic Fact
$60\overline{)240}$	$6 \times 10\overline{)24 \times 10}$	
$80\overline{)720}$		
$50\overline{)250}$		
$40\overline{)160}$		

Activity 7

A student entered the following problem on a calculator.

$8\overline{)59}$

Here is the answer the student got. | 0.14285714285714 |

1. Estimate what the answer should be by finding a near fact. _____

2. Find the exact answer on a calculator. _____

3. Describe the error the student made.

_____

_____

Unit 4

Name _____ Date _____

Unit Review
Measuring Two-Dimensional Objects

Activity 1

The drawing shows part of a skateboard ramp in a city park. About what size is it in square units?

Name _____ Date _____

Skills Maintenance
Counting Square Units

Activity 1

Find the area of each of the shapes by counting square units.

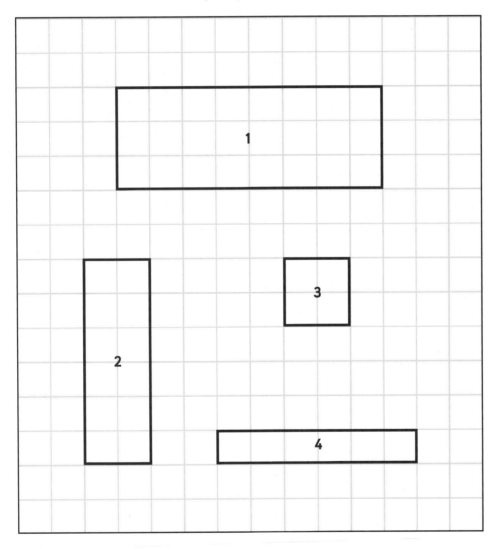

1. _____

2. _____

3. _____

4. _____

Name _____ Date _____

%÷ Apply Skills
=< x Arrays of Numbers 1 to 25

Activity 1

Write the dimensions of each of the rectangles.

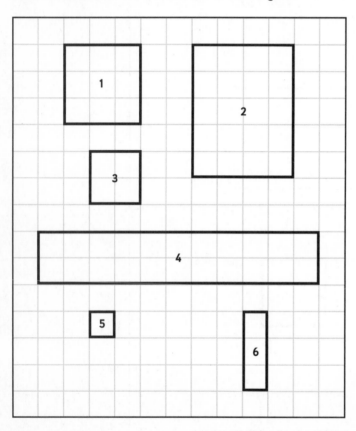

1. Dimensions _____ × _____

2. Dimensions _____ × _____

3. Dimensions _____ × _____

4. Dimensions _____ × _____

5. Dimensions _____ × _____

6. Dimensions _____ × _____

Name _____ Date _____

Problem-Solving Activity
Irregularly Shaped Objects

Use rectangles to estimate the number of square units in each object.
Draw rectangles inside and outside the object to get your estimate. Be
sure to multiply to figure out the number of square units.

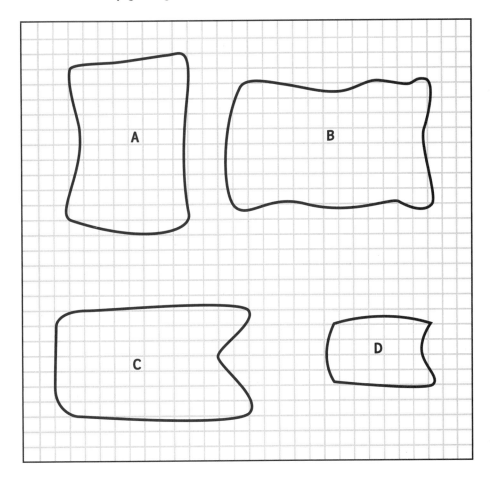

mBook Reinforce Understanding
Use the mBook *Study Guide* to review lesson concepts.

Unit 5 • Lesson 1   **183**

Name _____ Date _____

 Skills Maintenance
Basic Multiplication Facts

Activity 1

Solve the basic multiplication facts.

1. 3 × 4 _____

2. 2 × 6 _____

3. 2 × 9 _____

4. 3 × 6 _____

5. 3 × 8 _____

6. 4 × 6 _____

Name _____ Date _____

 Problem-Solving Activity
Area Formulas for Squares and Rectangles

Find the area of the shapes.

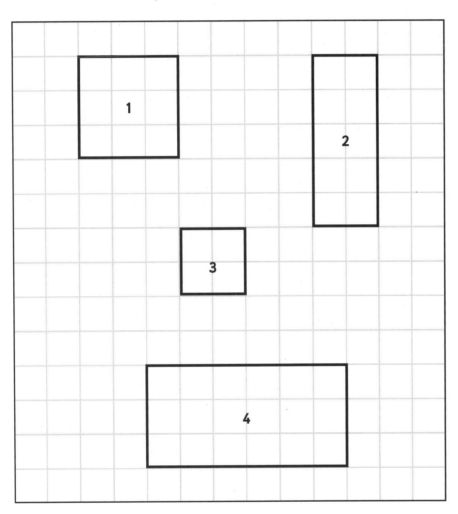

1. _____

2. _____

3. _____

4. _____

mBook **Reinforce Understanding**
Use the mBook *Study Guide* to review lesson concepts.

Name _____ Date _____

Skills Maintenance
Factors and Arrays

Activity 1

Fill in the dimensions of all arrays and factors for each number.

Number	Dimensions of Arrays	Factors
12	1×12 2×6 3×4	1, 2, 3, 4, 6, 12
18		
20		
23		
32		

Name _____ Date _____

 Apply Skills
From Arrays to Factors

| Activity 1 |

Use arrays to find the factors for the numbers.

1. Find the factors for the number 15.

   Write the factor list. _____

2. Find the factors for the number 20.

   Write the factor list. _____

Unit 5

Name _____ Date _____

 ## Problem-Solving Activity
Area Formulas for Triangles and Parallelograms

Find the areas of the triangles and parallelograms using area formulas.

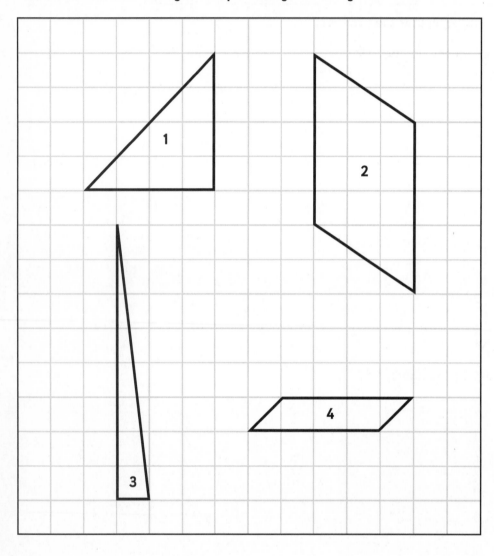

mBook **Reinforce Understanding**
Use the mBook *Study Guide* to review lesson concepts.

188 Unit 5 • Lesson 3

Name _____ Date _____

Skills Maintenance
Finding Factors

Activity 1

Circle the numbers in the list that are factors of the number given.

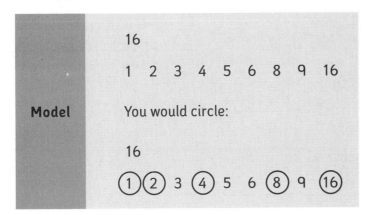

Model

16

1 2 3 4 5 6 8 9 16

You would circle:

16

①② 3 ④ 5 6 ⑧ 9 ⑯

1. 9

   1 2 3 4 5 7 9 11 18 27 36 45

2. 12

   1 2 3 4 5 6 7 11 12 13 15

3. 15

   1 3 5 7 9 11 13 15 17 19

Name _____ Date _____

 Apply Skills
Factor Rainbows

Activity 1

Draw factor rainbows for the numbers, then list all the factors.

Model	Draw the factor rainbow for the number 21.  1 3 7 21 The factors of 21 are 1, 3, 7, and 21.

1. Draw the factor rainbow for the number 16.

 The factors of 16 are _____.

2. Draw the factor rainbow for the number 15.

 The factors of 15 are _____.

3. Draw the factor rainbow for the number 12.

 The factors of 12 are _____.

4. Draw the factor rainbow for the number 7.

 The factors of 7 are _____.

Name _____ Date _____

 ### Problem-Solving Activity
Applying Area Formulas

The object below has a strange shape. Use what you know about the areas of squares, rectangles, and triangles to find the area of this object.

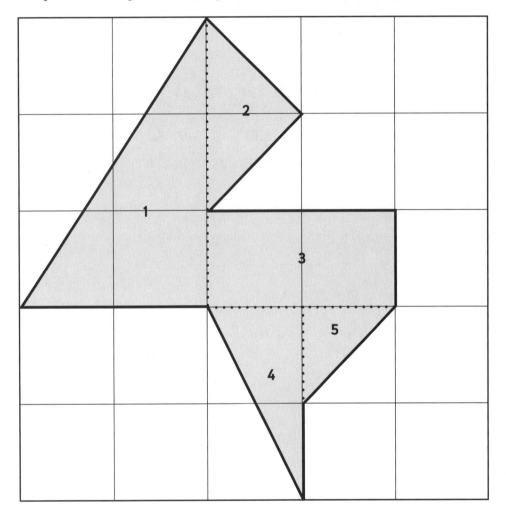

 mBook **Reinforce Understanding**
Use the mBook *Study Guide* to review lesson concepts.

Name _____ Date _____

Skills Maintenance
Finding Factors

Activity 1

Circle the numbers that are factors in the lists.

1. 27: 1 2 3 5 9 21 22 27 30

2. 32: 1 2 3 4 8 11 15 16 22 23 31 32 34

3. 40: 1 2 3 4 5 8 10 15 20 25 30 40 45 50

4. 9: 1 2 3 9 18 27 36 45

Name _____ Date _____

Apply Skills
Composite and Prime Numbers

Activity 1

Draw factor rainbows for the composite and prime numbers, and write their factor lists.

1. Draw the factor rainbow for the number 17.

   The factor list for 17 is _____.

2. Draw the factor rainbow for the number 21.

   The factor list for 21 is _____.

3. Draw the factor rainbow for the number 30.

   The factor list for 30 is _____.

4. Write a sentence that describes what prime numbers are.

   _____

   _____

   _____

mBook Reinforce Understanding
Use the mBook *Study Guide* to review lesson concepts.

Name _____ Date _____

 Skills Maintenance
Finding the Area

Activity 1

Give the area for each shape.

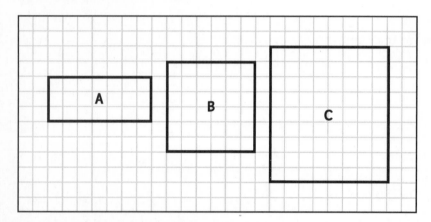

1. What is the area of shape A? _____

2. What is the area of shape B? _____

3. What is the area of shape C? _____

Name _____ Date _____

Apply Skills
Understanding Prime Numbers

Activity 1

The number grid shows all the whole numbers between 501 and 600.

There are 14 prime numbers between 501 and 600. Let's see if you can guess what some of them are. It would take a lot of lucky guesses to find all 14. However, you can make the task easier by crossing out numbers that you know are not prime.

Are there any numbers (or groups of numbers) that you can cross out right away—numbers that could not possibly be prime numbers? Use your pencil and cross out those numbers.

Write your reasons for crossing out these numbers (or for not crossing out other numbers).

501	502	503	504	505	506	507	508	509	510
511	512	513	514	515	516	517	518	519	520
521	522	523	524	525	526	527	528	529	530
531	532	533	534	535	536	537	538	539	540
541	542	543	544	545	546	547	548	549	550
551	552	553	554	555	556	557	558	559	560
561	562	563	564	565	566	567	568	569	570
571	572	573	574	575	576	577	578	579	580
581	582	583	584	585	586	587	588	589	590
591	592	593	594	595	596	597	598	599	600

_____

_____

_____

_____

_____

Name _____ Date _____

Problem-Solving Activity
Perimeter

Flor has five different vegetables planted in her backyard. Flor wants to put fencing around each of the patches. Answer the questions about perimeter. Each square on the grid has a base of 1 meter and a height of 1 meter.

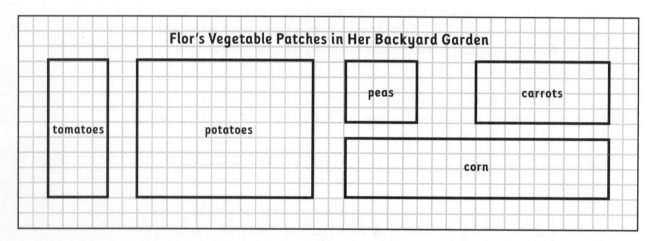

Flor's Vegetable Patches in Her Backyard Garden

1. How much fencing will Flor need for each vegetable patch (that is, what is the perimeter of each of the vegetable patches)?

   _____

   _____

2. How much bigger is the perimeter for the corn patch than the perimeter for the tomato patch?

   _____

   _____

3. Flor is thinking about getting rid of her carrot and pea patches. She wants to make her corn patch larger. It will still have a base of 18 meters, but it will now have a height of 8 meters. What will the perimeter for this new corn patch be?

   _____

   _____

mBook **Reinforce Understanding**
Use the mBook *Study Guide* to review lesson concepts.

Name _____ Date _____

Skills Maintenance
Prime Numbers

Activity 1

Circle all the prime numbers in the list.

2   3   5   6   9   11   13   15   22   29   31   35

Factors

Activity 2

List all of the factors for the numbers. The first is done for you.

Number	Factors
20	1, 2, 4, 5, 10, 20
12	
9	
13	
25	

Name _____ Date _____

%÷ Apply Skills
=< x Prime Factors

Activity 1

Fill in the factor trees with the missing numbers.

1. 250

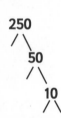

2. 75

3. 81

4. 100

5. 156

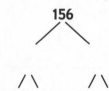

Name _____ Date _____

 Problem-Solving Activity
Different Shapes, Same Perimeter

Find the perimeter of each shape.

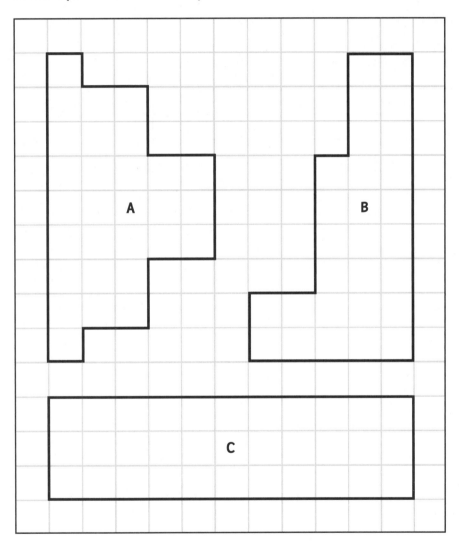

A. _____   B. _____   C. _____

 mBook Reinforce Understanding
Use the mBook *Study Guide* to review lesson concepts.

Name _____ Date _____

 Skills Maintenance
Factors

Activity 1

List all of the factors for each number. The first is done for you.

Number	Factors
10	1, 2, 5, 10
17	
2	
24	
8	
6	

Name _____ Date _____

 Apply Skills
More Practice on Prime Factor Trees

Activity 1

Draw prime factor trees for the numbers. Be sure to circle the prime factors.

1. Draw a prime factor tree for 18.

   The prime factorization of 18 is _____.

2. Draw a prime factor tree for 30.

   The prime factorization of 30 is _____.

Name _____ Date _____

Problem-Solving Activity
Same Perimeter, Different Area

Find the perimeter and the area for the shapes on the grid.

Perimeter _____
Area _____

Perimeter _____
Area _____

Perimeter _____
Area _____

mBook **Reinforce Understanding**
Use the mBook *Study Guide* to review lesson concepts.

202 Unit 5 • Lesson 8

Name _____ Date _____

Skills Maintenance
Factors

Activity 1

List all of the factors for each number. The first is done for you.

Number	Factors
9	1, 3, 9
45	
24	
42	
20	
36	

Unit 5

Name _____ Date _____

 ## Problem-Solving Activity
Comparing Area and Perimeter

Draw three rectangles of different sizes on the grid. Find the area and perimeter of each rectangle, and write the values next to the rectangles. Each square on the grid has a height of 1 cm and a base of 1 cm. Then answer the question.

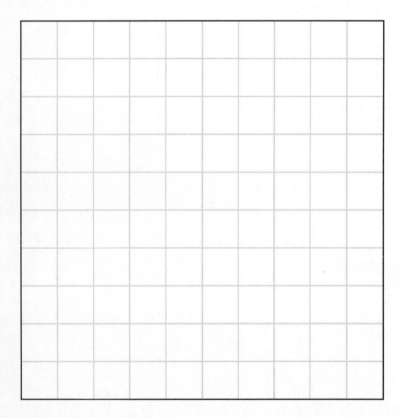

1. Is the area of a rectangle always bigger than the perimeter?

    _____

    _____

    _____

 mBook **Reinforce Understanding**
Use the mBook *Study Guide* to review lesson concepts.

Name _____ Date _____

Skills Maintenance
Prime Factorization

Activity 1

Complete the prime factor trees with the correct numbers. Then complete
the prime factorizations.

1. 81 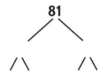 The prime factorization of 81 is

    _____ × _____ × _____ × _____ .

2. 80   The prime factorization of 80 is

    _____ × _____ × _____ × _____ × _____ .

3. 75   The prime factorization of 75 is

    _____ × _____ × _____ .

4. 60   The prime factorization of 60 is

    _____ × _____ × _____ × _____ .

5. 70   The prime factorization of 70 is

    _____ × _____ × _____ .

Name _____ Date _____

 ## Apply Skills
Common Errors in Prime Factorization

Activity 1

Look at the factor trees. Find the error, then correctly factor the number and describe your reasoning.

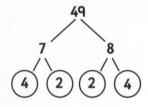

Describe the error.

_____

_____

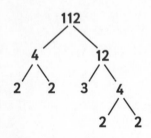

Describe the error.

_____

_____

mBook Reinforce Understanding
Use the mBook *Study Guide* to review lesson concepts.

Name _____ Date _____

 Skills Maintenance
Prime Factor Trees

Activity 1

Draw prime factor trees for the numbers.

1. 36

The prime factorization of 36 is _____ × _____ × _____ × _____ .

2. 50

The prime factorization of 50 is _____ × _____ × _____ .

3. 100

The prime factorization of 100 is _____ × _____ × _____ × _____ .

Unit 5

Name _____ Date _____

Apply Skills
Divisibility Rules for 2, 5, and 10

Activity 1

Write an X in the table if the dividing rule works for the number. More than one rule might work for a number. Mark all rules that work. Then complete Problems 1 through 3.

Number	Divide by 2	Divide by 5	Divide by 10
10	X	X	X
12			
15			
27			
65			
150			

1. Give an example of a five-digit number that you can divide by 2.

   _____

2. Give an example of a five-digit number that you can divide by 5.

   _____

3. Give an example of a five-digit number that you can divide by 10.

   _____

Name _____ Date _____

Problem-Solving Activity
Patterns in Area and Perimeter

Look closely at the table and answer the questions.

Rectangle	Base	Height	Difference Between Base and Height	Perimeter	Area
1	19	1	18	40	19
2	18	2	16	40	36
3	17	3	14	40	51
4	16	4	12	40	64
5	15	5	10	40	75
6	14	6	8	40	84
7	13	7	6	40	91
8	12	8	4	40	96
9	11	9	2	40	99
10	10	10	0	40	100

1. What happens to the area when the difference between the base and height gets smaller?

    _____

2. Of all of the rectangles, what shape has the largest area?

    _____

mBook Reinforce Understanding
Use the mBook *Study Guide* to review lesson concepts.

Name _____ Date _____

 Skills Maintenance
Basic Division Facts

Activity 1

Complete the basic division facts.

1. 10 ÷ 5 = _____   **2.** 16 ÷ 4 = _____   **3.** 18 ÷ 2 = _____

4. 35 ÷ _____ = 5   **5.** 10 ÷ 2 = _____   **6.** 28 ÷ _____ = 7

Name _____ Date _____

 Apply Skills
Divisibility Rules for 3 and 6

Activity 1

Write an X in the table if the divisibility rule works for the number. More than one rule might work for a number. Mark all rules that work. Then complete Problems 1 and 2.

Number	Divide by 3	Divide by 6
6	X	X
12		
15		
21		
24		
51		

1. Give an example of a four-digit number that you can divide by 3.

   _____

2. Give an example of a four-digit number that you can divide by 6.

   _____

Unit 5

Name _____ Date _____

 ## Problem-Solving Activity
Finding Area and Perimeter of Irregular Shapes

Find the area and perimeter for each shape.

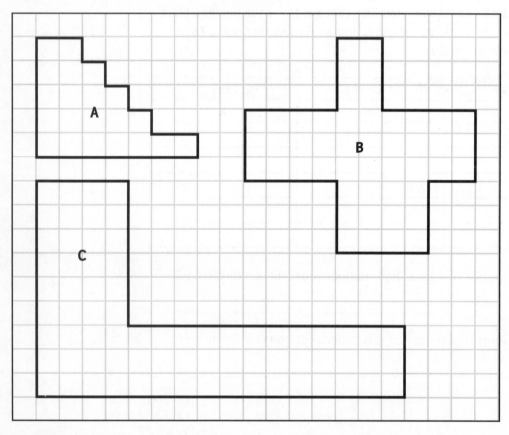

1. What is the area of shape A? _____

2. What is the area of shape B? _____

3. What is the area of shape C? _____

4. What is the perimeter of shape A? _____

5. What is the perimeter of shape B? _____

6. What is the perimeter of shape C? _____

mBook **Reinforce Understanding**
Use the mBook *Study Guide* to review lesson concepts.

Name _____ Date _____

 Skills Maintenance
Fact Families

Activity 1

Write fact families for the numbers.

1. 3, 7, 21

2. 8, 9, 72

3. 54, 9, 6

4. 63, 7, 9

Unit 5

Name _____ Date _____

Apply Skills
Practice with Divisibility Rules

Activity 1

Use the divisibility rules to fill in the table.

	Dividing Rules
2	We can divide a number by 2 if it is an even number.
3	We can divide a number by 3 if we can add up its digits and divide that number by 3 evenly.
5	We can divide a number by 5 if it ends in a 5 or a 0.
6	We can divide a number by 6 if we can divide it by 2 *and* by 3.
10	We can divide a number by 10 if it ends in a 0.

Number	Rule or Rules
270	**2, 3, 5, 6, and 10 rules**
555	
78	
393	
100	
666	

Cross out numbers that are not prime based on divisibility rules.

501	502	503	504	505	506	507	508	509	510
511	512	513	514	515	516	517	518	519	520
521	522	523	524	525	526	527	528	529	530
531	532	533	534	535	536	537	538	539	540
541	542	543	544	545	546	547	548	549	550
551	552	553	554	555	556	557	558	559	560
561	562	563	564	565	566	567	568	569	570
571	572	573	574	575	576	577	578	579	580
581	582	583	584	585	586	587	588	589	590
591	592	593	594	595	596	597	598	599	600

Name _____ Date _____

 Problem-Solving Activity
More Strategies for Finding Area

**The drawing on the grid shows a section of the design on a tile floor.
The pattern shows white and gray sections.**

1. What is the area of the gray center part of the pattern?

   _____

2. What is the area of the entire tile (the gray and white sections combined)?

   _____

3. What is the area of just the white border?

   _____

4. How do we use area formulas to find the area of the white border?

   _____

   _____

   _____

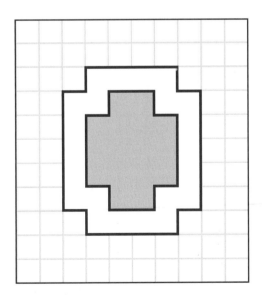

mBook Reinforce Understanding
Use the mBook *Study Guide* to review lesson concepts.

Name _____ Date _____

Skills Maintenance
Divisibility Rules

Activity 1

Write an X under each divisibility rule that applies to the numbers.

Number	by 2	by 3	by 5	by 6	by 10
27					
365					
402					
115					
782					
960					

Name _____ Date _____

Apply Skills
Prime Factorization for Large Numbers

Activity 1

Use dividing rules and a calculator to find the prime factors.

108

300

135

Name _____ Date _____

 ### Problem-Solving Activity
Looking for Patterns

The area of each square is the same. How many squares do you see in the checkerboard? The answer is not 64 or 65. It is much larger.

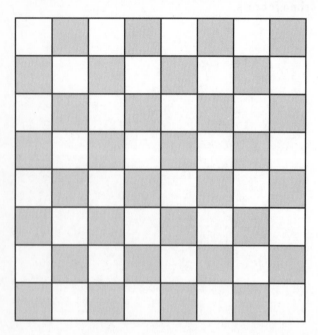

1. How many squares are there? _____

2. What strategy did you use to find them? _____

_____

_____

_____

_____

mBook Reinforce Understanding
Use the mBook *Study Guide* to review lesson concepts.

Name _____ Date _____

Skills Maintenance
Finding Arrays

Activity 1

Give the dimensions of each of the shapes.

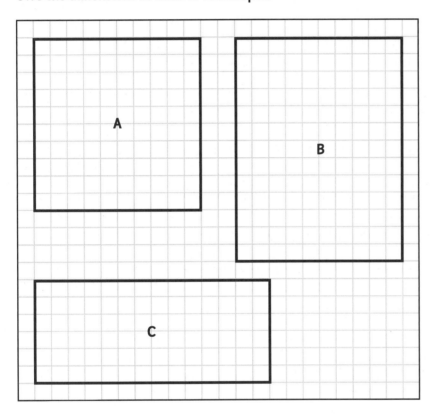

1. What are the dimensions of shape A? _____ × _____

2. What are the dimensions of shape B? _____ × _____

3. What are the dimensions of shape C? _____ × _____

Finding Primes

Activity 2

Circle the primes.

1 2 4 5 8 11 15 21 49

Name _____ Date _____

 Unit Review
Factors, Primes, and Composites

Activity 1

Circle the numbers in the list that are factors of the first number.

| Model | 12: ①②③④ 5 ⑥ 7 8 9 10 11 ⑫ 13 14 |

1. 8: 1 2 3 4 5 6 7 8 9 10 11 12 14 16

2. 15: 1 2 3 4 5 6 7 8 9 10 12 14 16 20

3. 20: 1 2 3 4 5 6 10 12 14 15 16 18 20 22 24

4. 27: 1 2 3 4 5 6 7 9 10 12 14 18 20 25 27 30 32

Activity 2

Tell whether the numbers are prime or composite by circling the correct response.

| Model | 7 ⟨prime⟩ or composite |

1. 9   prime or composite

2. 10   prime or composite

3. 19   prime or composite

4. 22   prime or composite

5. 37   prime or composite

Name _____ Date _____

Activity 3

Fill in the missing information in the prime factor trees. Then complete the prime factorization for each number.

Model

The prime factorization for 24 is 2 × 2 × 2 × 3.

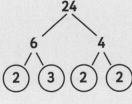

1. 18   The prime factorization for 18 is

    _____.

2. 25   The prime factorization for 25 is

    _____.

3. 28   The prime factorization for 28 is

    _____.

Activity 4

Put an X in the table if the dividing rule works for the number. The first problem is filled in as an example.

Number	by 2	by 3	by 5	by 6	by 10
615		X	X		
302					
650					
552					
112					

Name _____ Date _____

Unit Review
Area and Perimeter

Activity 1

Find the area and perimeter of the rectangles and/or squares with the given dimensions. Remember, area is measured in square units and perimeter in units.

Model	Base = 2 cm, Height = 5 cm Area ___10 sq cm___ Perimeter ___14 cm___

1. Base = 3 cm, Height = 4 cm

    Area _____   Perimeter _____

2. Base = 1 cm, Height = 3 cm

    Area _____   Perimeter _____

3. Base = 4 cm, Height = 2 cm

    Area _____   Perimeter _____

Activity 2

Find the area of the shapes. Remember, the area is measured in square units.

B. Area _____

C. Area _____

D. Area _____

E. Area _____

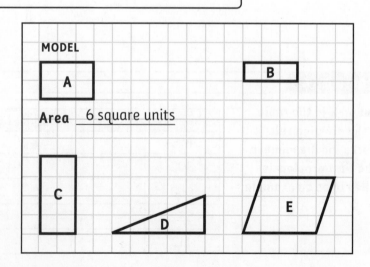

Name _____ Date _____

Activity 3

Change the rectangle into a square or rectangle that has the same perimeter but the largest possible area.

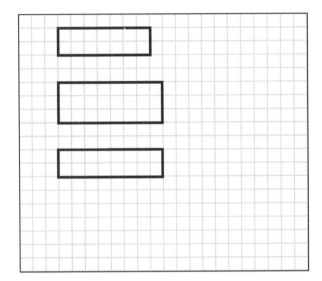

Activity 4

Change the objects into other objects that have the same areas but smaller perimeters.

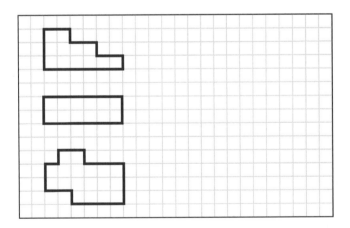

mBook **Reinforce Understanding**
Use the mBook *Study Guide* to review lesson concepts.

Name _____ Date _____

Skills Maintenance
Factors

Activity 1

Circle all the factors for each of the numbers.

1. 16 | 1 | 2 | 3 | 4 | 5 | 8 | 13 | 16 | 18 |

2. 21 | 1 | 2 | 3 | 5 | 7 | 9 | 11 | 21 | 24 |

3. 32 | 1 | 2 | 3 | 4 | 8 | 12 | 16 | 24 | 32 |

4. 49 | 1 | 3 | 5 | 7 | 9 | 11 | 22 | 33 | 49 |

5. 56 | 1 | 2 | 3 | 4 | 7 | 8 | 14 | 28 | 56 |

Name _____ Date _____

Apply Skills
Finding Common Factors

Activity 1

Do the following: 1) Draw an X through the factors for each number. List the factors. 2) Circle the factors the two numbers have in common. 3) List the numbers you have circled. These are the common factors.

1. 12

1	2	3	4	5	6	7	8	9	10	11	12	13	14	15

   15

1	2	3	4	5	6	7	8	9	10	11	12	13	14	15

   12 _____

   15 _____

   The common factors are _____.

2. 8

1	2	3	4	5	6	7	8	9	10	11	12	13	14	15

   12

1	2	3	4	5	6	7	8	9	10	11	12	13	14	15

   8 _____

   12 _____

   The common factors are _____.

Activity 2

List the factors of each number. Then find the common factor for each pair of numbers.

1. 21 _____

   42 _____

   Common factors _____

2. 81 _____

   18 _____

   Common factors _____

Name _____ Date _____

 Problem-Solving Activity
Classifying Shapes

Look at the shapes carefully. How are they alike? How are they different?

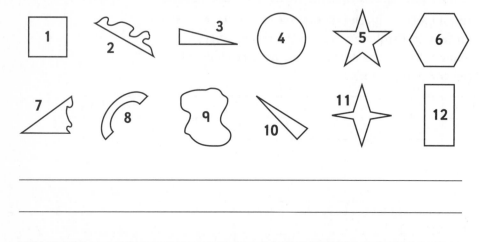

_____

_____

_____

Look for shapes that have at least one property in common. Make
between 5 and 7 groups. It is okay to have a shape by itself in a group.
Write the information about the shapes and groups in the table. You can
use each shape only once.

Group	Label for Group	Numbers for the Shapes in That Group	Describe What Is the Same About the Shapes in This Group
1			
2			
3			
4			
5			
6			
7			

mBook Reinforce Understanding
Use the mBook *Study Guide* to review lesson concepts.

Name _____ Date _____

Skills Maintenance
Factors

Activity 1

Circle all of the factors for each of the numbers.

1. 20 | 1 | 2 | 3 | 4 | 5 | 8 | 10 | 15 | 20 |

2. 18 | 1 | 2 | 3 | 4 | 6 | 9 | 12 | 15 | 18 |

3. 28 | 1 | 2 | 3 | 4 | 7 | 12 | 14 | 20 | 28 |

4. 42 | 1 | 2 | 3 | 4 | 6 | 7 | 14 | 21 | 42 |

5. 40 | 1 | 2 | 3 | 4 | 5 | 8 | 10 | 20 | 40 |

Unit 6

Name _____ Date _____

Apply Skills
More Practice Finding Common Factors

Activity 1

Do the following: 1) Draw an X through the factors for each number. List
the factors. 2) Circle all the factors the numbers have
in common. 3) List the numbers you have circled. These
are the common factors.

1.

15	1	2	3	4	5	6	7	8	9	10	11	12	13	14	15	16	17	18	19	20
20	1	2	3	4	5	6	7	8	9	10	11	12	13	14	15	16	17	18	19	20
25	1	2	3	4	5	6	7	8	9	10	11	12	13	14	15	16	17	18	19	20

15 _____

20 _____

25 _____

The common factors are _____.

2.

6	1	2	3	4	5	6	7	8	9	10	11	12	13	14	15	16	17	18	19	20
18	1	2	3	4	5	6	7	8	9	10	11	12	13	14	15	16	17	18	19	20
22	1	2	3	4	5	6	7	8	9	10	11	12	13	14	15	16	17	18	19	20

6 _____

18 _____

22 _____

The common factors are _____.

3.

12	1	2	3	4	5	6	7	8	9	10	11	12	13	14	15	16	17	18	19	20
24	1	2	3	4	5	6	7	8	9	10	11	12	13	14	15	16	17	18	19	20
36	1	2	3	4	5	6	7	8	9	10	11	12	13	14	15	16	17	18	19	20

12 _____

24 _____

36 _____

The common factors are _____.

Name _____ Date _____

 ## Problem-Solving Activity
Reclassifying Shapes

In the table, make at least three groups for the shapes. The shapes may appear in more than one group. Give a name to each shape group. Try to use each shape as many times as possible.

Group	Numbers for the Shapes In That Group	Describe What Is the Same About the Shapes in This Group
1		
2		
3		
4		
5		
6		
7		
8		
9		
10		
11		
12		

1 2 3 4 5 6

7 8 9 10 11 12

mBook Reinforce Understanding
Use the mBook *Study Guide* to review lesson concepts.

Unit 6

Name _____ Date _____

 ## Skills Maintenance
Factors

Activity 1

List all the factors for the numbers.

1. The factors of 6 are _____.

2. The factors of 18 are _____.

3. The factors of 25 are _____.

4. The factors of 32 are _____.

Activity 2

Answer the questions.

1. What are the common factors for 6 and 18? _____

2. What are the common factors for 18 and 32? _____

3. What are the common factors for 6 and 32? _____

Name _____ Date _____

 Apply Skills
Greatest Common Factor

Activity 1

Do the following: 1) List all of the factors for each number. 2) Circle all of the factors the two numbers have in common. 3) Tell which factor is the greatest common factor, or GCF.

1. 14 _____

   21 _____

14	1	2	3	4	5	6	7	8
21	1	2	3	4	5	6	7	8

   What is the largest number circled? _____

2. 5 _____

   20 _____

5	1	2	3	4	5	6	7	8
20	1	2	3	4	5	6	7	8

   What is the greatest common factor (GCF) of 5 and 20? _____

3. 14 _____

   18 _____

14	1	2	3	4	5	6	7	8
18	1	2	3	4	5	6	7	8

   What is the greatest common factor (GCF) of 14 and 18? _____

4. 8 _____

   12 _____

8	1	2	3	4	5	6	7	8
12	1	2	3	4	5	6	7	8

   What is the greatest common factor (GCF) of 8 and 12? _____

Name _____ Date _____

Problem-Solving Activity
Tessellations

In the last two lessons you classified shapes by looking at their properties. A good example of a design using the same properties over and over again is what is called a tessellation. These patterned drawings often use shapes that have straight lines, right angles, curves, and convex or concave properties.

Identify the shapes in the tessellation and their properties.

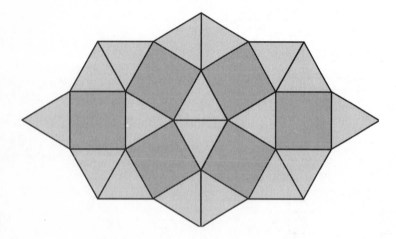

mBook Reinforce Understanding
Use the mBook *Study Guide* to review lesson concepts.

232 Unit 6 • Lesson 3

Name _____ Date _____

 Skills Maintenance
Factors

Activity 1

List all the factors.

1. The factors of 9 are _____.

2. The factors of 12 are _____.

3. The factors of 16 are _____.

4. The factors of 25 are _____.

Unit 6

Name _____ Date _____

 Apply Skills
More Practice With the GCF

Activity 1

Do the following: 1) List all of the factors for each number. 2) Circle all
of the factors the two numbers have in common. 3) Tell
which factor is the greatest common factor, or GCF.
4) List the fact families that correspond with the GCF.

1. 10 _____

    25 _____

    30 _____

10	1	2	3	4	5	6	7	8
25	1	2	3	4	5	6	7	8
30	1	2	3	4	5	6	7	8

What is the GCF of 10, 15, and 30? _____

Multiplication and division fact families _____

_____

2. 6 _____

    18 _____

    24 _____

6	1	2	3	4	5	6	7	8
18	1	2	3	4	5	6	7	8
24	1	2	3	4	5	6	7	8

What is the GCF of 6, 18, and 24? _____

Multiplication and division fact families _____

_____

Name _____ Date _____

Problem-Solving Activity
Congruent Shapes

Look at the patterns. All of the shapes are congruent, they are just rotated in different directions. Draw the shape that comes next in the patterns.

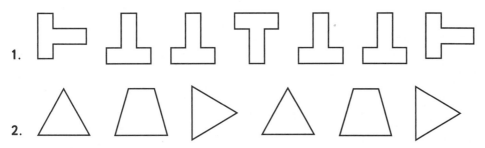

1.

2.

Now use the worksheet on the next page and make a pattern using one or two congruent shapes. The pattern can have a maximum of 10 shapes. Make a plan in the space below first. Be prepared to share your pattern with classmates after you are finished to see if they can predict the next shape.

Name _____ Date _____

mBook **Reinforce Understanding**
Use the mBook *Study Guide* to review lesson concepts.

236 Unit 6 • Lesson 4

Name _____ Date _____

Skills Maintenance
Finding the GCF

Activity 1

Find the GCF for the pairs of numbers.

1. What is the GCF of 18 and 20? _____

2. What is the GCF of 24 and 28? _____

3. What is the GCF of 32 and 36? _____

4. What is the GCF of 12 and 48? _____

Congruent Shapes

Activity 2

In each row of shapes, there is one shape that is congruent. Circle it.

1.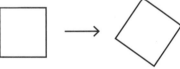

2.

3.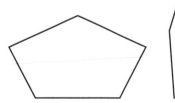

4.

Name _____ Date _____

 Apply Skills
Prime Factor Trees and the GCF

Activity 1

Make prime factor trees for the pairs of numbers, and find the GCF.

1. What is the GCF of 66 and 90? _____

2. What is the GCF of 24 and 36? _____

3. What is the GCF of 30 and 25? _____

mBook Reinforce Understanding
Use the mBook *Study Guide* to review lesson concepts.

Name _____ Date _____

Skills Maintenance
GCF

Activity 1

Find the GCF for each pair of numbers.

1. What is the GCF of 18 and 20? _____

2. What is the GCF of 15 and 30? _____

3. What is the GCF of 24 and 38? _____

4. What is the GCF of 40 and 50? _____

Name _____ Date _____

Apply Skills
More Practice With Prime Factor Trees and the GCF

Activity 1

Find the greatest common factor of these two numbers. Use prime factor trees to find the GCF.

1. Find the greatest common factor of 120 and 150.

- Circle pairs or prime numbers in the factor trees.

- For each of the trees, multiply all of the numbers that you have circled to get the greatest common factor. If there's only one number, then that is the greatest common factor.

The greatest common factor of 120 and 150 is _____.

2. Find the greatest common factor of 90 and 105.

- Circle pairs of prime numbers in the factor trees.

- For each of the trees, multiply all of the numbers that you have circled to get the greatest common factor. If there's only one number, then that is the greatest common factor.

The greatest common factor of 90 and 105 is _____.

Name _____ Date _____

Problem-Solving Activity
Making Congruent Shapes

Look at the shape. It looks like the letter L. Show how many ways you can divide the shape using different congruent shapes. More space is provided on the next page.

Name _____ Date _____

mBook **Reinforce Understanding**
Use the mBook *Study Guide* to review lesson concepts.

242   Unit 6 • Lesson 6

Name _____ Date _____

Skills Maintenance
GCF

Activity 1

Find the GCF for the pairs of numbers. List the factors of each number.

1. 4 and 8 _____

   _____

   _____

2. 16 and 18 _____

   _____

   _____

3. 20 and 40 _____

   _____

   _____

4. 25 and 50 _____

   _____

   _____

Name _____ Date _____

%÷ Apply Skills
≡< X Even and Odd Numbers

Activity 1

Think about the kinds of numbers you get when you add or multiply the numbers in the chart. Do not solve the problems. Just put an X in the box to indicate whether the answer to the problem will be even or odd. The first problem is done for you.

Problem	Even Number	Odd Number
6,349 + 76,945	X	
987 + 1,854		
889 × 935		
93,456 + 123,554		
773 + 595		
87 × 359		
328,340 + 222		
132,602 × 67		
22,421 + 648,448		
393 × 107		

Name _____ Date _____

Problem-Solving Activity
Similarity

Each square in this grid has a base of 1 centimeter and a height of 1 centimeter. Draw a rectangle that has a base of 4 centimeters and a height of 2 centimeters. Next, make two more rectangles. One rectangle should have a base and height that are both 3 times larger than in your original rectangle. The next rectangle should have a base and height that are both half as large as in your original rectangle. Label your rectangles 1, 2, and 3, then fill in the table below the grid.

	Rectangle	Perimeter	Area
1			
2			
3			

mBook Reinforce Understanding
Use the mBook *Study Guide* to review lesson concepts.

Name _____ Date _____

Skills Maintenance
GCF

Activity 1

Find the GCF for these numbers. List the factors for each number.

1.   12, 18, 24   _____

_____

_____

_____

2.   48 and 64   _____

_____

_____

3.   18, 27, 81   _____

_____

_____

_____

4.   120 and 160   _____

_____

_____

5.   17, 19, 23   _____

_____

_____

_____

Name _____ Date _____

 ## Apply Skills
Square Numbers

> **Activity 1**

Look at the lists of numbers. Tell if they are (a) odd numbers, (b) even numbers, (c) square numbers, or (d) consecutive whole numbers. All you need to write on the line is a, b, c, or d.

1. What are these numbers? _____

    1 2 3 4 5 6 7 8 9 10

2. What are these numbers? _____

    1 3 5 7 9 11 13 15 17 19

3. What are these numbers? _____

    1 4 9 16 25 36 49 64 81 100

4. What are these numbers? _____

    2 4 6 8 10 12 14 16 18 20

5. What are these numbers? _____

    25 27 29 31 33 35 37 39 41 43

6. What are these numbers? _____

    25 36 49 64 81 100 121 144 169 196

Name _____ Date _____

 Problem-Solving Activity
The Geometry of Square Numbers

Start with the square in the upper left corner of the grid. It has a base of
1 cm and a height of 1 cm. Now draw a square in the upper left corner of
the grid that has a base that is 1 centimeter bigger and a height that is
1 centimeter bigger than the first square. It will overlap the first square.
The new square will have a base of 2 centimeters and a height of 2
centimeters. Keep going until you have drawn 10 squares, each one
1 centimeter in base and 1 centimeter in height bigger than the one
before it.

After drawing the squares list the size of each square on a separate piece
of paper. Find the area. Then find the difference in area between each two
consecutive squares.

mBook **Reinforce Understanding**
Use the mBook *Study Guide* to review lesson concepts.

Name _____ Date _____

 Skills Maintenance
Common Factors and GCF

Activity 1

Tell the common factors for each set.

1. 8 and 24 _____

2. 12 and 18 _____

3. 10, 12, 20 _____

4. 15, 35, 45 _____

5. 8, 12, 16, 18 _____

Activity 2

Tell the GCF for each set.

1. 4, 16, 24 _____

3. 24, 26, 28 _____

2. 156 and 64 _____

4. 120 and 180 _____

Name _____ Date _____

%÷ Apply Skills
Square Numbers and Odd Numbers

Activity 1

Tell how many squares should be added to get the next consecutive square number in each problem. Draw a picture and shade the squares that you are adding to get from one square number to the next.

Model	1	4	9	16
	□	How many added? ___3___	How many added? ___5___	How many added? ___7___

1. 25

How many added? _____

2. 36

How many added? _____

3. 49

How many added? _____

Name _____ Date _____

 ### Problem-Solving Activity
Expanding and Contracting Triangles

On the grid, use what you know about triangles to expand or contract the triangle. Expand the first two triangles, and contract the last two triangles.

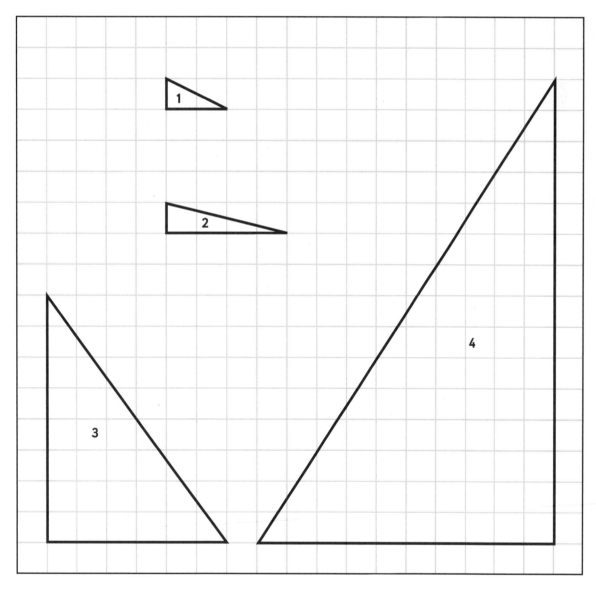

mBook Reinforce Understanding
Use the mBook *Study Guide* to review lesson concepts.

Name _____ Date _____

Skills Maintenance
Factors

Activity 1

Make factor lists for the numbers.

1. 12 _____

2. 36 _____

3. 35 _____

4. 42 _____

5. 18 _____

6. 21 _____

Name _____ Date _____

Unit Review
Common Factors and Number Patterns

Activity 1

Create factor trees for the numbers. Then make a list of the factors and circle the GCF.

1. 52 _____

    130 _____

2. 63 _____

    84 _____

3. 81 _____

    117 _____

Activity 2

Decide if the answers to the problems will be even or odd using the rules you learned. Do not work the problems.

1. $54 + 63$ _____ 2. 64×63 _____

3. $72 \div 4$ _____ 4. $37 - 11$ _____

5. $37 + 9$ _____ 6. $102 \div 3$ _____

7. 55×3 _____ 8. $110 \div 2$ _____

Name _____ Date _____

Activity 3

Continue adding square blocks to the picture so that you get bigger and bigger square arrays. Each time you make a square array, go to the table and fill in this information: 1) the number the array represents, 2) description of the array, 3) the number of blocks in the array, 4) the number of blocks you added to make the square number.

The beginning of the table is filled in for you.

Number the Array Represents	Description of the Array	Number of Blocks in the Array	Number of Blocks You Added
1	1 × 1	1	1
4	2 × 2	4	3

Name _____ Date _____

Unit Review
Properties of Shapes, Congruence, and Similarity

Activity 1

On a blank sheet of paper, classify the shapes into four different groups, based on their properties. Shapes may be used more than once.

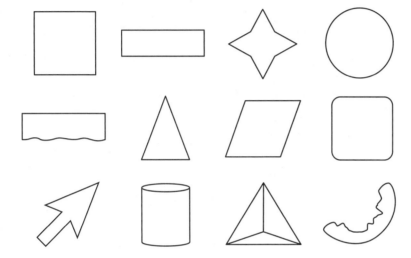

Activity 2

Circle the shape in each group that is not congruent to the others.

1.

2.

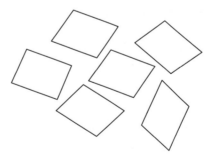

3.

Name _____ Date _____

Activity 3

Find either the expanded or contracted forms of the triangle. Write the number you multiplied or divided by and draw the triangle on the grid.

1. Contract _____

2. Expand _____

3. Expand _____

4. Contract _____

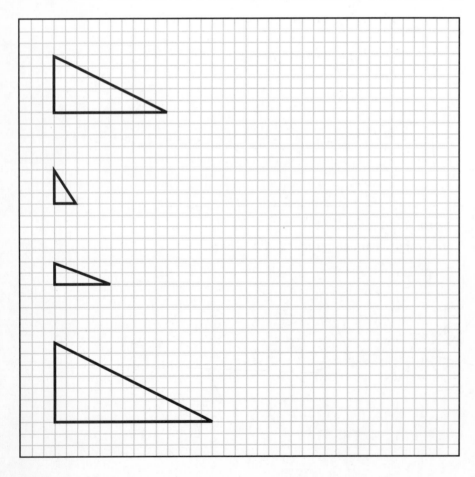

mBook **Reinforce Understanding**
Use the mBook *Study Guide* to review lesson concepts.

Name _____ Date _____

Skills Maintenance
Consecutive Multiplication Facts

Activity 1

Solve the multiplication problems.

1. $4 \cdot 1$ _____
2. $4 \cdot 2$ _____
3. $4 \cdot 3$ _____

4. $4 \cdot 4$ _____
5. $4 \cdot 5$ _____
6. $6 \cdot 3$ _____

7. $6 \cdot 4$ _____
8. $6 \cdot 5$ _____
9. $6 \cdot 6$ _____

10. $6 \cdot 7$ _____
11. $7 \cdot 6$ _____
12. $7 \cdot 7$ _____

13. $7 \cdot 8$ _____
14. $7 \cdot 9$ _____
15. $7 \cdot 10$ _____

Name _____ Date _____

%÷ Apply Skills
Working With Triangular Numbers

Activity 1

Look at the pictures of consecutive triangular numbers and fill in the missing information in the table. The first row of the table has been completed as a model. You may use a calculator.

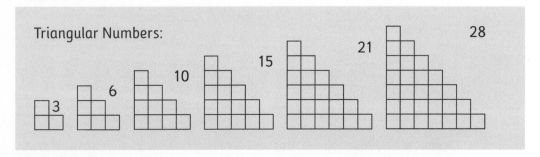

Triangular Numbers:

3   6   10   15   21   28

How many squares?	8 times the number of squares + 1	Check for square numbers
3	3 × 8 + 1 = 25	5 × 5 = 25
		7 × 7 =
		9 × 9 =
		11 × 11 =
		13 × 13 =
		15 × 15 =

Name _____ Date _____

Problem-Solving Activity
Tangrams

Cut out the tangram pieces. Try making your own designs with the pieces.
The sunset and the candle are two designs you can make from tangrams.
Be sure to save your tangram pieces for future lessons.

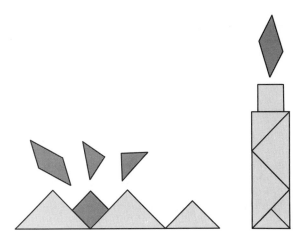

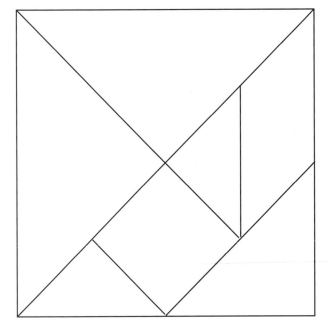

mBook Reinforce Understanding
Use the mBook *Study Guide* to review lesson concepts.

This page intentionally left blank.

Name _____ Date _____

Skills Maintenance
Basic Multiplication

Activity 1

Solve the consecutive multiplication facts.

1. 6 · 2 _____

2. 6 · 3 _____

3. 6 · 4 _____

4. 6 · 5 _____

5. 6 · 6 _____

6. 7 · 4 _____

7. 7 · 5 _____

8. 7 · 6 _____

9. 7 · 7 _____

10. 7 · 8 _____

11. 9 · 6 _____

12. 9 · 7 _____

13. 9 · 8 _____

14. 9 · 9 _____

15. 9 · 10 _____

Activity 2

Look at the number line. What is it counting by? Fill in the missing numbers.

1.

0   5   ___ ___ ___ ___ ___   35

2.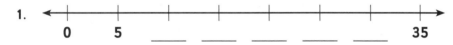

24   ___ ___ ___ ___ ___   60

3.

21   ___ ___ ___ ___ ___ ___   70

4.

24   ___ ___ ___ ___ ___ ___   80

Name _____ Date _____

Apply Skills
Exponents

Activity 1

Rewrite the multiplication problems using exponents.

1. $5 \cdot 5 \cdot 5 \cdot 5$ _____

2. $2 \cdot 2 \cdot 2 \cdot 5$ _____

3. $3 \cdot 3 \cdot 3 \cdot 3 \cdot 5$ _____

4. $10 \cdot 10 \cdot 10 \cdot 10 \cdot 10 \cdot 10 \cdot 10 \cdot 10 \cdot 10$ _____

5. $2 \cdot 3 \cdot 3 \cdot 3$ _____

Activity 2

Write the numbers using repeated multiplication.

1. 3^2 _____

2. 7^4 _____

3. 9^3 _____

4. $2 \cdot 3^2$ _____

5. $5 \cdot 4^4$ _____

Name _____ Date _____

 Problem-Solving Activity
More Tangrams

In the last lesson, you cut out tangram pieces and made some designs of your own. Today you will be copying designs from the book. See how many of the designs you can make using some or all your tangram shapes.

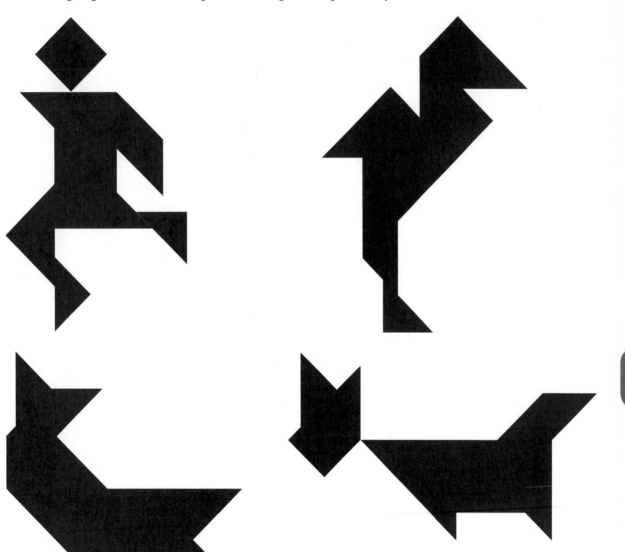

mBook Reinforce Understanding
Use the mBook *Study Guide* to review lesson concepts.

Unit 7

Name _____ Date _____

 Skills Maintenance
Exponents

Activity 1

Rewrite as powers.

1. $2 \cdot 2 \cdot 2 \cdot 2 \cdot 2 \cdot 2$ _____

2. $3 \cdot 3 \cdot 3$ _____

3. $5 \cdot 5$ _____

4. $10 \cdot 10 \cdot 10 \cdot 10 \cdot 10 \cdot 10 \cdot 10$ _____

5. $7 \cdot 7 \cdot 7 \cdot 7$ _____

Name _____ Date _____

 Apply Skills
Patterns With Exponents

Activity 1 [_____]

Multiply the powers.

1. $10^7 \times 10^3$ _____

2. $7^4 \times 7^3$ _____

3. $5^2 \times 5$ _____ (Remember, 5 is the same as 5^1)

4. $3^2 \times 3^{10}$ _____

5. $4^3 \times 4^2$ _____

6. $2^6 \times 2^9$ _____

Unit 7

This page intentionally left blank.

Name _____ Date _____

 ## Problem-Solving Activity
Slides, Flips, and Turns

Look at the pictures. Find the tangram piece that matches each gray shape on the left and trace it on your grid paper. Then move the shape in the same way it is moved in the picture (a flip, a slide, or a turn) and trace the shape to match the shape on the right.

Model

You will be given a picture like this:

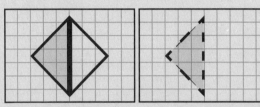

First, find your tangram triangle that matches. Put it on the blank grid paper, and trace it (page 269).

Then look at the picture to see how it was moved. In the picture above, the shape was flipped. Flip your triangle the same way, and trace it again like in the picture.

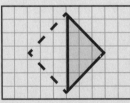

Your finished drawing will look like this.

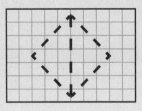

Name _____ Date _____

Now it is your turn to copy some designs. Be sure to move the shapes the same way as shown in the picture. Trace the shapes on your grid paper using your tangram pieces. You should use the medium triangle for Problem 3.

1.

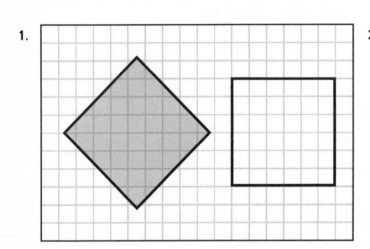

2.

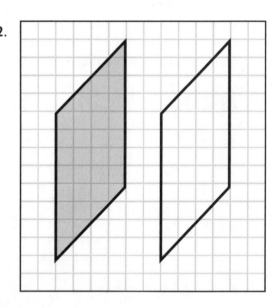

3.

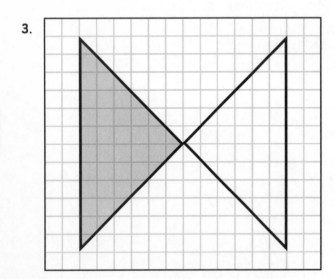

Name _____ Date _____

1.

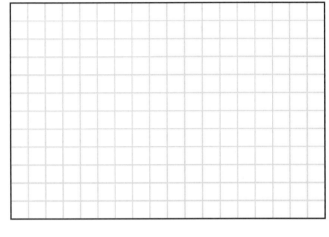

2.

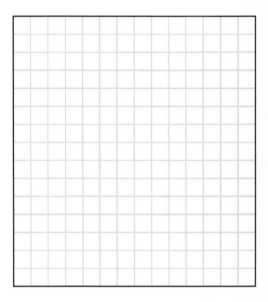

3.

mBook **Reinforce Understanding**
Use the mBook *Study Guide* to review lesson concepts.

Unit 7 • Lesson 3   **269**

Name _____ Date _____

 Skills Maintenance
Exponents

Activity 1

Rewrite the numbers using exponents.

Model	$2 \times 2 \times 2 \times 2 \times 2$ $\underline{2^5}$

1. $4 \times 4 \times 4 \times 4 \times 4$ _____

2. $30 \times 30 \times 30 \times 30 \times 30$ _____

3. $8 \times 3 \times 3$ _____

4. $10 \times 9 \times 9 \times 9 \times 9 \times 9 \times 9$ _____

5. $6 \times 8 \times 8$ _____

Name _____   Date _____

Apply Skills
More Exponent Patterns

Activity 1

Multiply the powers.

Model	$10^4 \times 100^1 = 10^4 \times 10^2 = 10^4 + 10^2$ $\underline{10^6}$

1. $10^2 \times 1,000^1$ _____
   (Remember: $1,000^1 = 10^3$)

2. $100^1 \times 10^6$ _____
   (Remember: $100^1 = 10^2$)

3. $9^2 \times 9^9$ _____

4. $12^5 \times 12^5$ _____

5. $10^1 \times 10,000^1$ _____
   (Remember: $10,000^1 = 10^4$)

6. $100^1 \times 100^1$ _____
   (Remember: $100^1 = 10^2$)

Name _____ Date _____

Problem-Solving Activity
Symmetry

Circle the objects that have a correctly drawn line of symmetry.
Then redraw the other objects in the grid, correctly drawing a line of symmetry if possible.

1.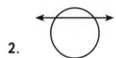

2.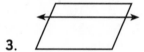

3.

4.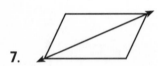

5.

6.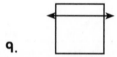

7.

8.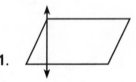

9.

10.

11.

12.

Name _____ Date _____

Skills Maintenance
Slides, Flips, and Turns

Activity 1

Tell whether each move is a slide, flip, or turn.

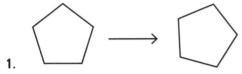

1. _____

2. _____

3. _____

4. _____

5. _____

6. _____

7. _____

Unit 7

Name _____ Date _____

%÷=<x **Apply Skills**
Common Multiples

Activity 1

Write the first five multiples of each number. Start each list by rewriting the number itself.

1. 7   _____ _____ _____ _____ _____

2. 9   _____ _____ _____ _____ _____

3. 5   _____ _____ _____ _____ _____

4. 2   _____ _____ _____ _____ _____

5. 10   _____ _____ _____ _____ _____

Activity 2

Using the number lines, find common multiples for each pair of numbers and list them.

1. Find common multiples of 2 and 3. _____

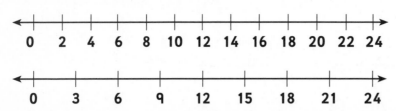

2. Find common multiples of 5 and 10. _____

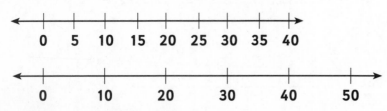

3. Find common multiples of 6, 8, and 12. _____

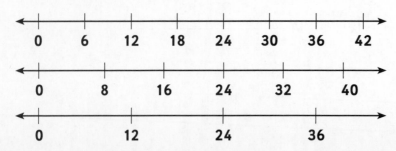

Name _____ Date _____

 Skills Maintenance
Symmetry and Movement of Shapes

Activity 1

Draw a line of symmetry through each of the objects.

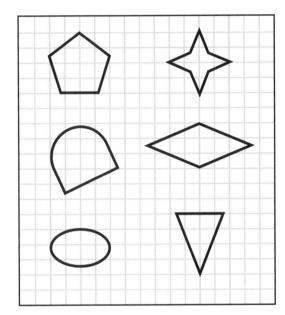

Activity 2

Circle slide, flip, or turn to describe the movements of the shapes.

1. Slide   Flip   Turn

2. Slide   Flip   Turn

3. Slide   Flip   Turn

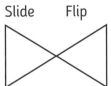

4. Slide   Flip   Turn

5. Slide   Flip   Turn

6. Slide   Flip   Turn

Unit 7

Name _____ Date _____

%÷ **Apply Skills**
Least Common Multiple (LCM)

Activity 1

Make organized lists to find the least common multiple (LCM) of the numbers. When you find the least common multiple, circle it.

1. What is the least common multiple (LCM) of 5 and 10? _____

   5 | _____ |

   10 | _____ |

2. What is the least common multiple (LCM) of 2 and 7? _____

   2 | _____ |

   7 | _____ |

3. What is the least common multiple (LCM) of 3 and 4? _____

   3 | _____ |

   4 | _____ |

Activity 2

Tuned In is a new computer game. The sound part of the game is difficult, because you have to press the space bar on the computer keyboard every time different sounds happen at the same time.

1. At the easy level of the game, the player hears a horn every 5 seconds and a whistle every 3 seconds. When will be the first time that the player will hear the horn and whistle at the same time?

   _____

   _____

2. The hardest level of the game also has three sounds. The whistle goes off every 3 seconds, the horn goes off every 6 seconds, and bang occurs every 8 seconds. When do they all go off at the same time?

   _____

   _____

Name _____ Date _____

Problem-Solving Activity
Symmetry and Mobiles

Circle the property or properties shown in each of the mobile designs.

1. Circle all the properties that apply:

    Flip   Slide   Turn

    Congruence   Symmetry

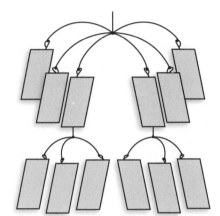

2. Circle all the properties that apply:

    Flip   Slide   Turn

    Congruence   Symmetry

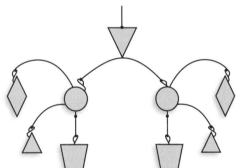

3. Circle all the properties that apply:

    Flip   Slide   Turn

    Congruence   Symmetry

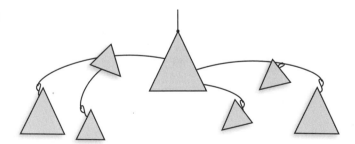

mBook Reinforce Understanding
Use the mBook *Study Guide* to review lesson concepts.

Unit 7

Name _____ Date _____

Skills Maintenance
Least Common Multiples

Activity 1

Write the first ten multiples of each number. Then find the least common multiple.

Model										
10	10	20	30	40	50	(60)	70	80	90	100
12	12	24	36	48	(60)	72	84	96	108	120

1. 5   _____ _____ _____ _____ _____ _____ _____ _____ _____ _____

    3   _____ _____ _____ _____ _____ _____ _____ _____ _____ _____

2. 8   _____ _____ _____ _____ _____ _____ _____ _____ _____ _____

    4   _____ _____ _____ _____ _____ _____ _____ _____ _____ _____

3. 9   _____ _____ _____ _____ _____ _____ _____ _____ _____ _____

    2   _____ _____ _____ _____ _____ _____ _____ _____ _____ _____

4. 6   _____ _____ _____ _____ _____ _____ _____ _____ _____ _____

    7   _____ _____ _____ _____ _____ _____ _____ _____ _____ _____

Name _____ Date _____

 ## Problem-Solving Activity
Creating Mobiles

Draw a sketch of a mobile on the grid. Use one or more types of objects for your mobile. Show slides, flips, or turns for the objects. Decide whether the mobile will or will not have symmetry.

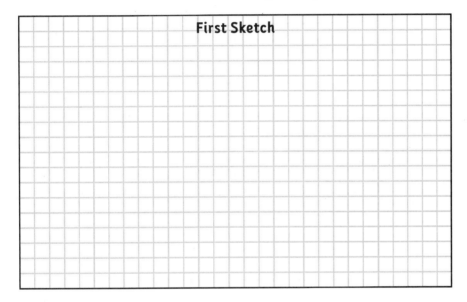

First Sketch

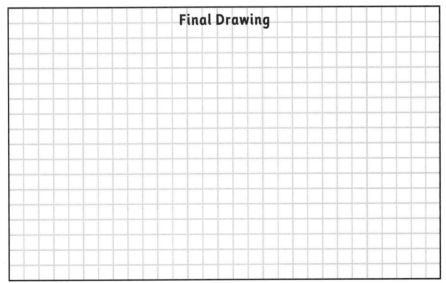

Final Drawing

 mBook **Reinforce Understanding**
Use the mBook *Study Guide* to review lesson concepts.

Name _____ Date _____

 Skills Maintenance
Slides, Flips, and Turns

Activity 1

Circle slide, flip, or turn to describe the movements of the shapes.

1. Slide   Flip   Turn

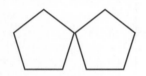

2. Slide   Flip   Turn

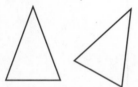

3. Slide   Flip   Turn

4. Slide   Flip   Turn

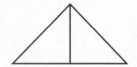

Name _____ Date _____

Apply Skills
Applications of LCM

Activity 1

We have set the two wheels on our cuckoo clock to turn at different rates. Your job is to figure out the least common multiple. It is the time when the wheels meet.

1. number of hours for
    one complete turn
    6
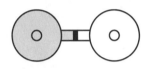
    number of hours for
    one complete turn
    9

What is the least common multiple? _____

2. number of hours for
    one complete turn
    7
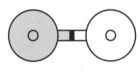
    number of hours for
    one complete turn
    4

What is the least common multiple? _____

3. number of hours for
    one complete turn
    5
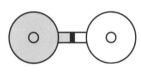
    number of hours for
    one complete turn
    8

What is the least common multiple? _____

4. number of hours for
    one complete turn
    4
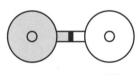
    number of hours for
    one complete turn
    10

What is the least common multiple? _____

Name _____ Date _____

 Problem-Solving Activity
Rotational Symmetry

Circle the objects that have rotational symmetry.

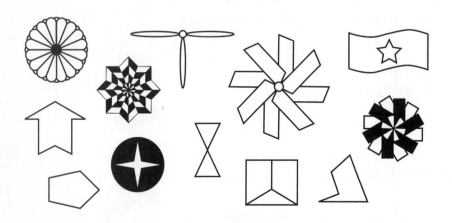

Now select one of the objects that does not have rotational symmetry. Draw it on the grid so that it has rotational symmetry.

mBook **Reinforce Understanding**
Use the mBook *Study Guide* to review lesson concepts.

282 Unit 7 • Lesson 8

Name _____ Date _____

Skills Maintenance
Symmetry and LCM

Activity 1

Tell whether the objects have symmetry. Circle yes or no.

1. This object has rotational symmetry.   yes   no

2. This object has rotational symmetry.   yes   no

3. This object has a line of symmetry.   yes   no

4. This object has a line of symmetry.   yes   no

Activity 2

When will the wheels on the cuckoo clock meet?

1.   number of hours for one complete turn   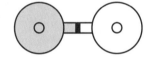   number of hours for one complete turn

    [2]   [8]

What is the least common multiple? _____

2.   number of hours for one complete turn   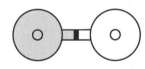   number of hours for one complete turn

    [3]   [7]

What is the least common multiple? _____

3.   number of hours for one complete turn   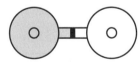   number of hours for one complete turn

    [5]   [15]

What is the least common multiple? _____

Unit 7

Name _____ Date _____

 Apply Skills
Properties of Numbers

Activity 1

Show at least four different ways of writing or describing each number.
Use what you've learned about odd, even, prime, and composite numbers.
Include dividing rules, multiples, factors, and patterns in addition and
multiplication.

Model	14	$14 = 10 + 4$ It is a composite number. It is a multiple of 7.	It is an even number. We can divide by 2. It is a multiple of 2.

36   9

37   90

Name _____ Date _____

 ## Problem-Solving Activity
More Rotational Symmetry

Draw one unique object that has rotational symmetry and one that does not have rotational symmetry.

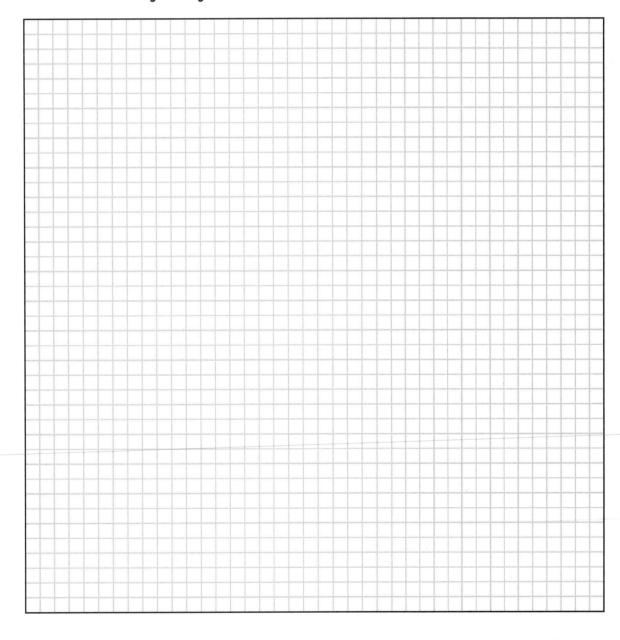

mBook **Reinforce Understanding**
Use the mBook *Study Guide* to review lesson concepts.

Name _____ Date _____

 Skills Maintenance
Basic Multiplication

Activity 1

Complete the multiplication facts.

1. 7 · 1 _____   2. 7 · 2 _____

3. 7 · 3 _____   4. 7 · 4 _____

5. 7 · 5 _____   6. 9 · 3 _____

7. 9 · 4 _____   8. 9 · 5 _____

9. 9 · 6 _____   10. 9 · 7 _____

Activity 2

Look at the number line. What is it counting by? Fill in the missing numbers.

1.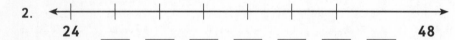

0   4   ___ ___ ___ ___ ___ ___ ___   36

2.

24   ___ ___ ___ ___ ___ ___ ___   48

3.

33   ___ ___ ___ ___ ___ ___ ___   121

4.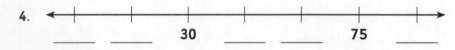

___ ___   30   ___ ___   75   ___

Name _____ Date _____

Unit Review
Number Patterns and Common Multiples

Activity 1

Use each triangular number to find a square number.

Model	3	$3 \times 8 = 24$	$24 + 1 = 25$

1. 6 _____   **2.** 10 _____   **3.** 1 _____   **4.** 15 _____

Activity 2

Multiply the exponents.

1. $100^1 \cdot 10^3$ _____   **2.** $6^4 \cdot 6^2$ _____   **3.** $8^3 \cdot 8$ _____
(Remember, 8 is the same as 8^1)

Activity 3

List 10 multiples for each number. Put a circle around the common multiples. Write the least common multiple.

Model	4	4	8	12	16	20	24	28	32	36	40
	5	5	10	15	20	25	30	35	40	45	50
	LCM	20									

1. 2 _____ _____ _____ _____ _____ _____ _____ _____ _____ _____

   3 _____ _____ _____ _____ _____ _____ _____ _____ _____ _____

   LCM _____

2. 6 _____ _____ _____ _____ _____ _____ _____ _____ _____ _____

   9 _____ _____ _____ _____ _____ _____ _____ _____ _____ _____

   LCM _____

Name _____ Date _____

A third wheel has been added to our cuckoo clock. You need to think about all three numbers to find the least common multiple.

1.   number of hours for   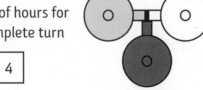   number of hours for
          one complete turn   one complete turn

                     4   3

               number of hours for
               one complete turn

                    6

What is the least common multiple? _____

Show at least four different ways of writing or describing the number.

Model	
	12 12 = 10 + 2. It is an even number. It is a composite number. We can divide by 2. It is a multiple of 6. It is a multiple of 2.

35

_____

_____

17

_____

_____

81

_____

_____

Name _____ Date _____

 Unit Review
Symmetry

Activity 1

Each of the shapes has been moved. Tell whether each move was a slide, flip, or turn. Then identify whether the shapes have line symmetry, rotational symmetry, or both.

1. _____

   symmetry _____

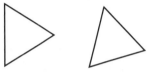

2. _____

   symmetry _____

3. _____

   symmetry _____

4. _____

   symmetry _____

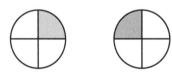

Activity 2

Use at least three of the shapes above to create a design on the grid. You can use any shape more than once. You can also slide, flip, or turn them.

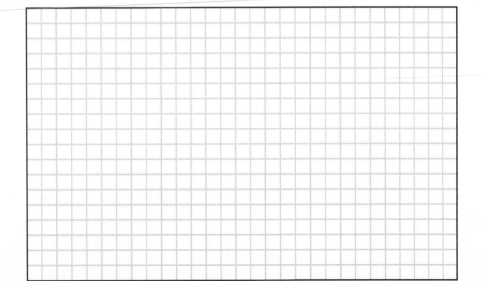

Unit 7

Name _____ Date _____

 Skills Maintenance
Number Lines

Activity 1

Fill in the missing whole numbers on the number lines.

1.

3   _____   _____   6   7

2.

298   299   _____   _____   302

3.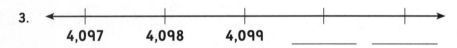

4,097   4,098   4,099   _____   _____

Name _____ Date _____

 Apply Skills
Fractional Parts on a Number Line

Activity 1

Fill in the missing halves on the number lines. Fill in decimal numbers above the number line and fractions below the number line.

1.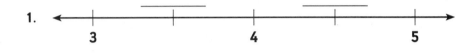

3   4   5

2.

199   200   201

3.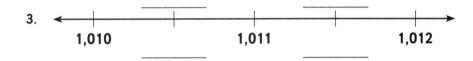

1,010   1,011   1,012

Activity 2

Fill in the missing thirds on the number lines. Fill in decimal numbers above the number line and fractions below the number line.

1.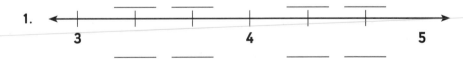

3   4   5

2.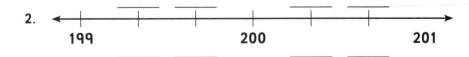

199   200   201

3.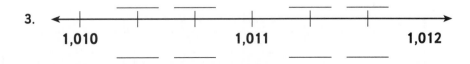

1,010   1,011   1,012

Name _____ Date _____

 ## Problem-Solving Activity
Finding Averages

Roll two dice five different times and record the data for each roll. Make
a bar graph to show the data. The first graph should have bars showing
the sums for each of the five rolls. On the second graph, show how you
can rearrange the bars so that they are about even.

Sum									
12									
11									
10									
9									
8									
7									
6									
5									
4									
3									
2									
1									
	first roll		second roll		third roll		fourth roll		fifth roll

Sum									
12									
11									
10									
9									
8									
7									
6									
5									
4									
3									
2									
1									
	first roll		second roll		third roll		fourth roll		fifth roll

Name _____ Date _____

 ## Skills Maintenance
Fractions and Decimal Numbers on a Number Line

Activity 1

Fill in the missing fractions, decimal numbers, and whole numbers on the number lines. Fill in decimal numbers above the number line and fractions below the number line.

Model

4.00   4.50   5.00   5.50   6.00

4   4$\frac{1}{2}$ 5   5$\frac{1}{2}$ 6

1.
12.50   12.75

12   12$\frac{1}{2}$ 12$\frac{3}{4}$ 13

2.
49.33

49   49$\frac{1}{3}$

3.
77.00   78.00   79.00

77   78   79

4.
3.50   3.75

3   3$\frac{1}{2}$ 3$\frac{3}{4}$

5.
129.33

129   129$\frac{1}{3}$

Unit 8

Name _____ Date _____

Apply Skills
Fractional and Decimal Number Parts Between 0 and 1

| Activity 1 |

Divide each of the number lines into equal parts of the fractions given.

1. Halves

0   1

2. Fourths

0   1

3. Thirds

0   1

4. Sixths

0   1

Name _____ Date _____

Problem-Solving Activity
Estimating Averages

For each graph, draw a line where you think the average will be. Then redistribute the bars until you find an average. Cross out parts of some bars and add shading to others.

Problem 1									
12									
11									
10							▓		
9							▓		
8		▓					▓		
7		▓					▓		
6		▓					▓		
5	▓						▓		
4	▓						▓		▓
3	▓		▓		▓		▓		▓
2	▓		▓		▓		▓		▓
1	▓	▓	▓	▓	▓	▓	▓	▓	▓

Name _____ Date _____

Problem 2								
120								
110								
100								
90								
80								
70								
60								
50								
40								
30								
20								
10								

mBook Reinforce Understanding
Use the mBook *Study Guide* to review lesson concepts.

Name _____ Date _____

 Skills Maintenance
Fractions and Decimal Numbers Between 0 and 1

Activity 1

Answer the questions about fractions and decimal numbers between 0 and 1. Write the decimal numbers above the number line and fractions below the number line.

1. If you divide the segment of the number line between 0 and 1 into thirds, name the fractions and decimal numbers you would find in between:

2. If you divide the segment of the number line between 0 and 1 into fourths, name the fractions and decimal numbers you would find in between:

3. If you divide the segment of the number line between 0 and 1 into halves, name the fractions and decimal numbers:

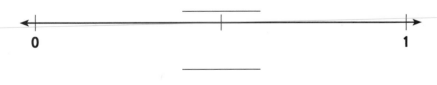

Unit 8

Name _____ Date _____

÷ Apply Skills
Fair Shares

Activity 1

Divide the shapes into the fractional parts specified.

1. Divide the circle into fourths.

2. Divide the square into thirds.

3. Divide the hexagon into halves.

Activity 2

Divide the shapes. Notice how the same fractional part can look very different from one shape to the next.

1. Divide the objects into thirds.

2. Divide the objects into fifths.

3. Divide the objects into fourths.

Name _____ Date _____

 Problem-Solving Activity
Computing the Mean and the Range

Imagine that you are trying to find a place to live where the weather is mostly the same all year. Look at the chart. You are given temperatures for 11 days of the year for three different cities. Use your calculator to find the mean, minimum, maximum, and range in temperature for each city. Then answer the questions.

El Sol, Arizona	Tiempo, New Mexico	San Tropo, California
65	38	75
98	120	94
120	96	81
122	78	82
68	33	92
77	112	80
59	91	94
72	114	84
66	98	86
119	90	88
80	87	90
Mean	Mean	Mean
Minimum	Minimum	Minimum
Maximum	Maximum	Maximum
Range	Range	Range

What city would you choose? _____

What information did you rely on the most for making your decision?

_____

_____

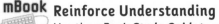

mBook Reinforce Understanding
Use the mBook *Study Guide* to review lesson concepts.

Unit 8

Name _____ Date _____

Skills Maintenance
Fractions and Decimal Numbers Between 0 and 1

Activity 1

Divide the number lines into fair shares of the given fractional part. Label the parts with fractions and decimal numbers.

1. Halves

    20   21

2. Fourths

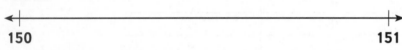

    150   151

3. Thirds

    0   1

Name _____ Date _____

Apply Skills
Identifying the Numerator and Denominator

Activity 1

For each problem, write the total parts and the parts we have. Then tell whether each is the numerator or denominator by circling the correct term.

1. $\frac{7}{8}$ Total parts _____   Numerator   or   Denominator

      Parts we have _____   Numerator   or   Denominator

2. $\frac{6}{8}$ Total parts _____   Numerator   or   Denominator

      Parts we have _____   Numerator   or   Denominator

3. $\frac{2}{10}$ Total parts _____   Numerator   or   Denominator

      Parts we have _____   Numerator   or   Denominator

Activity 2

Draw the fractions using circles and rectangles. Remember, the denominator tells you the total parts, and the numerator is the part you shade.

Fraction	Circle	Rectangle
Model $\frac{1}{3}$		
$\frac{3}{4}$		
$\frac{3}{6}$		
$\frac{1}{4}$		

Unit 8

Name _____ Date _____

Problem-Solving Activity
The Median in Data

Measure the height (in inches) of nine students in your class. Record the data in Table 1. Calculate the mean, median, minimum, maximum, and range of the nine students. Record your calculations in Table 2.

Next pretend that four professional basketball players just joined your class and they want to be measured too. They all play center for their teams. Here are their heights.

Johnson—85 inches
Williams—83 inches
McKee—87 inches
Jamaal—81 inches

Add the four basketball players to Table 1. Then calculate the mean, median, minimum, maximum, and range of all 13 students. Record your calculations in Table 3.

Table 1	
Student Name	**Height (in inches)**
1	
2	
3	
4	
5	
6	
7	
8	
9	
10	
11	
12	
13	

Table 2: Statistics Without Basketball Players	
Mean	
Median	
Minimum	
Maximum	
Range	

Table 3: Statistics Including Basketball Players	
Mean	
Median	
Minimum	
Maximum	
Range	

Name _____ Date _____

 ## Skills Maintenance
Identifying the Numerator and Denominator

Activity 1

For each problem, write the total parts or the parts we have. Then tell whether each is the numerator or denominator by circling the correct term.

1. $\frac{8}{9}$

    Total parts _____   Numerator   or   Denominator

2. $\frac{1}{32}$

    Parts we have _____   Numerator   or   Denominator

3. $\frac{10}{71}$

    Parts we have _____   Numerator   or   Denominator

4. $\frac{5}{1}$

    Total parts _____   Numerator   or   Denominator

Unit 8

Name _____ Date _____

Problem-Solving Activity
Outliers in Data

In the last lesson, you recorded the heights of the students in your class and professional basketball players. You also calculated the mean, median, minimum, maximum, and range for the two different groups. Look at the tables in the last lesson and do the following on a separate sheet of paper:

1. Re-record the heights of the students in your class. List the heights from shortest to tallest.

2. Re-record the statistics for the class without the basketball players.

3. Re-record the heights of the students in your class and the professional basketball players. List the heights from shortest to tallest.

4. Re-record the statistics for the class including the basketball players.

Use the tables to answer the questions.

5. List any outliers in the data.

    Heights Without Basketball Players:

    _____

    Heights Including Basketball Players:

    _____

6. How was the range affected by including the heights of the basketball players? Why?

    _____

    _____

7. How was the mean affected by including the heights of the basketball players? Why?

    _____

    _____

Name _____ Date _____

 ### Skills Maintenance
Identifying the Numerator and Denominator

| Activity 1 |

For each problem, write the total parts or the parts we have. Then tell whether each is the numerator or denominator by circling the correct term.

1. $\dfrac{7}{8}$

   Total parts _____   Numerator   or   Denominator

2. $\dfrac{16}{19}$

   Total parts _____   Numerator   or   Denominator

3. $\dfrac{1}{81}$

   Parts we have _____   Numerator   or   Denominator

4. $\dfrac{9}{10}$

   Parts we have _____   Numerator   or   Denominator

5. $\dfrac{7}{1}$

   Total parts _____   Numerator   or   Denominator

Unit 8

Name _____ Date _____

Apply Skills
Fractions Less Than, Equal To, and Greater Than 1

Activity 1

Draw a picture of each of the fractions. Tell whether the fractions are less than, equal to, or greater than 1 by circling the appropriate phrase.

1. $\frac{9}{5}$ Circle one: less than 1   equal to 1   greater than 1

   Draw a picture using one or more fraction bars.

2. $\frac{3}{4}$ Circle one: less than 1   equal to 1   greater than 1

   Draw a number line.

3. $\frac{6}{6}$ Circle one: less than 1   equal to 1   greater than 1

   Draw a picture using a circle or circles.

4. $3\frac{3}{8}$ Circle one: less than 1   equal to 1   greater than 1

   Draw a picture using a square or squares.

Activity 2

Write the improper fractions as whole numbers.

1. $\frac{4}{2}$ _____   2. $\frac{9}{3}$ _____   3. $\frac{15}{3}$ _____

4. $\frac{20}{5}$ _____   5. $\frac{16}{2}$ _____   6. $\frac{4}{4}$ _____

Name _____ Date _____

 Problem-Solving Activity
Comparing Tables of Data

Three classes at Big Lake Elementary School decide to have a long jump contest. The teachers select five students from each sixth-grade class to be in the contest. The tables show how far each student jumped. All distances are in inches.

Find the mean, median, and range for the distances jumped for each class. Use the rewrite column to put the distances in order. Then answer the questions.

Schultz	(rewrite)
25	
59	
68	
72	
66	

Fernandez	(rewrite)
46	
45	
52	
52	
50	

Rivera	(rewrite)
74	
33	
37	
31	
35	

Mean	
Median	
Range	

Mean	
Median	
Range	

Mean	
Median	
Range	

1. On average, which class jumped the farthest? _____

2. On average, which class jumped the least far? _____

3. Which class had the biggest difference between its longest and shortest jump?

   _____

4. Compare the ranges for each of the three classes. How does range affect mean and median?

   _____

   _____

   _____

Unit 8

Name _____ Date _____

 Skills Maintenance
Fractional Parts

Activity 1

Divide the shapes correctly into halves.

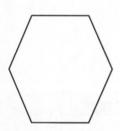 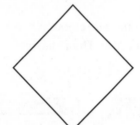  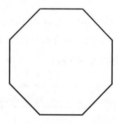

Activity 2

Complete the fraction to make it equal to 1.

1. $\dfrac{}{4} = 1$

2. $\dfrac{3}{} = 1$

3. $\dfrac{16}{} = 1$

4. $\dfrac{2}{2} = $ _____

Name _____ Date _____

Apply Skills
Estimating Fractional Parts

Activity 1

Estimate the size of the fractional parts shown in each problem. You may use either fraction or decimal number benchmarks.

1.

0   1

Estimate _____

2.

0   1

Estimate _____

3.

0   1

Estimate _____

4.

0   1

Estimate _____

5.

0   1

Estimate _____

6.

0   1

Estimate _____

Unit 8

Name _____ Date _____

 Problem-Solving Activity
Comparing Tables in Data

Each table lists the distance (in miles) each of the students in Mr. Johnson's class has to travel to get to school. Use a calculator to find the mean, median, range, and outliers for the students on each bus. Use your calculations to answer the questions.

Bus A	Bus B	Bus C
4	7	2
7	8	5
9	9	6
9	9	9
11	10	11
13	10	12
15	13	13
20	14	14
Mean: Median: Range: Outliers:	Mean: Median: Range: Outliers:	Mean: Median: Range: Outliers:

1. On average, which group of students travels the farthest?

   _____

2. Which group of students has the biggest difference between the student who travels the farthest and the student who travels the least far? What is the difference?

   _____

3. Which group of students has the most accurate mean? Why?

   _____

   _____

   _____

   _____

Name _____ Date _____

 ### Skills Maintenance
Fractional Parts

Activity 1

Estimate the fractional part that is shaded. You may give your answer as a fraction or decimal number benchmark.

1.

Estimate _____

2.

Estimate _____

Activity 2

Determine the number represented by the rectangles.

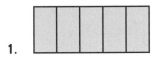 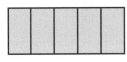 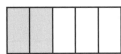

1.

Answer _____

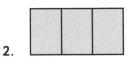 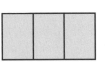 

2.

Answer _____

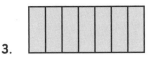 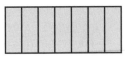  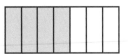

3.

Answer _____

Unit 8

Name _____ Date _____

 Apply Skills
Surveying Students—Fractions and Statistics

Activity 1

Channel 5 has five kinds of shows. The table shows how many 30-minute segments are aired for each kind of show. Find the fractional portion of airtime each kind of show represents. To get your fractions, you will first have to find the total number of 30-minute segments Channel 5 aired.

Type	Number of 30-Minute Segments	Fraction of Segments
Sports	18	
Sitcoms	35	
Soap Operas	30	
News	14	
Cartoons	28	

Name _____ Date _____

Problem-Solving Activity
Stem-and-Leaf Plots

Use a ruler to give an estimated length of your classmates' hair. Write the data in the column. Then take the information and put it in a stem-and-leaf plot.

Column of Data	Stem-and-Leaf Plot	
Lengths		

1. What is the range of the data?

   _____

2. Where are most of the numbers?

   _____

mBook **Reinforce Understanding**
Use the mBook *Study Guide* to review lesson concepts.

Name _____ Date _____

Skills Maintenance
Estimating Fractional Parts

Activity 1

Estimate the fractional part that is shaded. Write your answer in both fraction and decimal number form.

1.

Fraction _____   Decimal Number _____

2.

Fraction _____   Decimal Number _____

3.

Fraction _____   Decimal Number _____

4.

Fraction _____   Decimal Number _____

Name _____ Date _____

 Apply Skills
Estimating Fractional Parts on a Number Line

> **Activity 1**

Look at the dot on each number line and estimate its location by thinking about the closest fraction or decimal number benchmark.

1.

0   1   2

Estimate _____

2.

4   5   6

Estimate _____

3.

7   8   9

Estimate _____

4.

0   1   2

Estimate _____

5.

9   10   11

Estimate _____

6.

250   251   252

Estimate _____

Unit 8

Name _____ Date _____

 Problem-Solving Activity
Creating Stem-and-Leaf Plots

Use the table on *Student Text*, page 507, to find the data to make a
stem-and-leaf plot. It should show the number of baseball games lost.
Remember you are to use only the numbers in the column that's labeled
Losses. Include all the teams. Be careful, you will not be using the
other information in the table for this activity. You are just using the
information about losses. Create your stem-and-leaf plot on the following
page. Once you are finished, answer the questions.

Model	Here's how we break apart numbers in the hundreds for a stem-and-leaf plot.

127 →

Tens	Ones
12	7

12 tens is equal to 120 and then we add 7 more to
get 127.

Name _____ Date _____

Make observations about your stem-and-leaf plot.

1. Where are the most losses? _____

2. What is the range? _____

mBook **Reinforce Understanding**
Use the mBook *Study Guide* to review lesson concepts.

Name _____ Date _____

 Skills Maintenance
Estimating Fractions

Activity 1

Estimate the fractional parts that are shaded. Use both fraction and decimal number benchmarks.

1. Fraction _____ Decimal Number _____

2. Fraction _____ Decimal Number _____

3. Fraction _____ Decimal Number _____

4. Fraction _____ Decimal Number _____

Name _____ Date _____

 Apply Skills
Comparing Fractions: Which One Is Bigger?

Activity 1

Draw circles to help you decide which fraction is bigger in each pair. The drawings help you visualize the fractional parts, but they don't have to be exact. Put a check next to the larger fraction.

1. $\frac{3}{4}$ $\frac{1}{2}$ 2. $\frac{7}{8}$ $\frac{1}{8}$ 3. $\frac{2}{3}$ $\frac{1}{2}$

4. $\frac{1}{3}$ $\frac{3}{4}$ 5. $\frac{3}{4}$ $\frac{1}{8}$

Activity 2

Shade the fraction bars to compare each pair of fractions. Then tell which fraction is bigger.

1. Compare $\frac{8}{9}$ and $\frac{3}{5}$. Which is bigger? _____

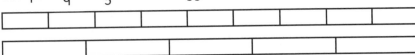

2. Compare $\frac{4}{8}$ and $\frac{5}{9}$. Which is bigger? _____

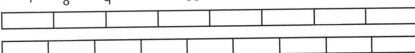

3. Compare $\frac{1}{16}$ and $\frac{2}{3}$. Which is bigger? _____

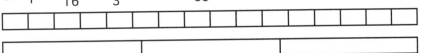

4. Compare $\frac{5}{6}$ and $\frac{5}{7}$. Which is bigger? _____

mBook Reinforce Understanding
Use the mBook *Study Guide* to review lesson concepts.

Unit 8

Name _____ Date _____

 ## Skills Maintenance
Fractions and Decimal Numbers

Activity 1

Put a check mark next to the larger fraction in each pair. You may use circles to help you visualize the fractions.

1. $\frac{4}{5}$ $\frac{1}{5}$

2. $\frac{1}{3}$ $\frac{2}{3}$

3. $\frac{1}{2}$ $\frac{2}{3}$

4. $\frac{3}{4}$ $\frac{1}{2}$

5. $\frac{7}{8}$ $\frac{2}{8}$

Activity 2

Write the decimal number benchmarks for each of these fractions.

1. $\frac{1}{2}$ _____

2. $\frac{3}{4}$ _____

3. $\frac{1}{3}$ _____

4. $\frac{2}{3}$ _____

5. $\frac{1}{4}$ _____

Name _____ Date _____

Apply Skills
Fraction Bars

Activity 1

Find what fraction is represented by each fraction bar.

1. What fraction? _____

2. What fraction? _____

   What fraction? _____

2. What fraction? _____

   What fraction? _____

   What fraction? _____

3. What fraction? _____

   What fraction? _____

   What fraction? _____

Name _____ Date _____

 Problem-Solving Activity
Finding the Median on a Stem-and-Leaf Plot

Imagine that Tyrone Jackson is the top fullback for a professional football team. The team won enough games to make it into the playoffs, but they lost their first playoff game. The chart shows which games the team won and lost. It also shows how many yards Jackson rushed in each game. Make a stem-and-leaf plot of the yards Jackson rushed in the 17 games, then use a calculator to answer the questions.

Game	Score	Won or Lost	Yards Rushed by Jackson
1	17–7	Won	41
2	21–3	Won	75
3	17–14	Lost	34
4	24–10	Won	99
5	31–3	Lost	34
6	10–7	Lost	32
7	28–21	Won	156
8	17–10	Lost	41
9	34–21	Lost	39
10	21–17	Won	163
11	14–3	Won	42
12	10–0	Won	78
13	24–21	Won	79
14	20–7	Won	77
15	10–7	Lost	37
16	21–0	Won	77
play-off	27–17	Lost	35

Name _____ Date _____

	Stems	Leaves

1. What was the mean number of yards rushed? _____

2. Circle the median in the stem-and-leaf plot.

   What was the median? _____

3. What was the range? _____

mBook **Reinforce Understanding**
Use the mBook *Study Guide* to review lesson concepts.

Name _____ Date _____

 ## Skills Maintenance
Comparing Fractions: Which One Is Bigger?

Activity 1

Put a check mark next to the larger fraction in each pair. You may use circles to help visualize the fractions.

1. $\dfrac{10}{12}$ $\dfrac{3}{12}$

2. $\dfrac{10}{12}$ $\dfrac{1}{2}$

3. $\dfrac{1}{2}$ $\dfrac{7}{8}$

4. $\dfrac{1}{2}$ $\dfrac{1}{8}$

5. $\dfrac{3}{4}$ $\dfrac{1}{8}$

Name _____ Date _____

Apply Skills
Equivalent Fractions

Activity 1

Identify the equivalent fractions in the fraction bars.

1.

The equivalent fractions are $\frac{1}{3}$ and _____ $\frac{2}{3}$ and _____.

2.

The equivalent fractions are $\frac{2}{6}$ and _____ $\frac{4}{6}$ and _____.

Activity 2

Choose two of the fraction bars in each problem. Identify equivalent fractions by shading the two bars. Then write the equivalent fractions.

1.

What are the equivalent fractions?

_____

_____

Activity 3

Draw fraction bars for each fraction, and shade them to show they are equivalent.

1. $\frac{1}{3}$

$\frac{2}{6}$

2. $\frac{1}{2}$

$\frac{2}{4}$

Name _____ Date _____

Problem-Solving Activity
Line Plots

This table shows the results of the long jump at a national college competition. We rounded off the distance each person jumped to the nearest foot. Make a line plot that shows how far these 10 people jumped.

Jumper	Longest Distance for the Day
Williams	23
McCoy	27
Owens	22
Johnson	22
Wong	26
Hernandez	23
Rios	22
Lemore	24
Clemons	26
Barber	25

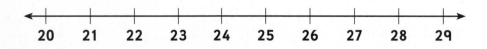

1. What is the range? _____

2. What is the most common distance? _____

mBook Reinforce Understanding

Use the mBook *Study Guide* to review lesson concepts.

Name _____ Date _____

 ## Skills Maintenance
Line Plots and Statistics

Activity 1

Answer the questions using the line plot.

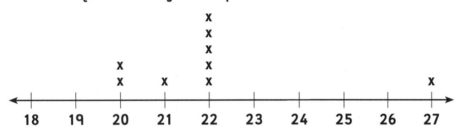

1. What is the range? _____

2. What is the most common number? _____

3. What is the outlier? _____

Activity 2

Find the average of this data set.

10   9   2   6   8

Answer _____

Name _____ Date _____

%÷ **Apply Skills**
≤ x **Identifying Equivalent Fractions**

Activity 1

Show equivalent fractions using a number line or fraction bar.

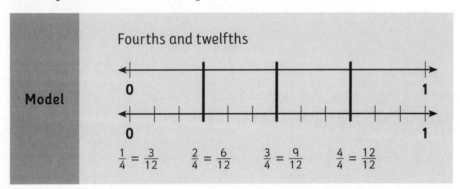

Model

Fourths and twelfths

$\frac{1}{4} = \frac{3}{12}$ $\frac{2}{4} = \frac{6}{12}$ $\frac{3}{4} = \frac{9}{12}$ $\frac{4}{4} = \frac{12}{12}$

1. Thirds and twelfths

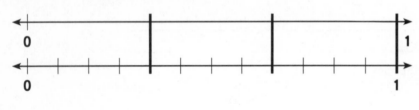

_____ = _____   _____ = _____

2. Halves and twelfths

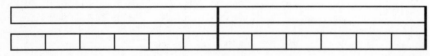

_____ = _____   _____ = _____

3. Thirds and Sixths

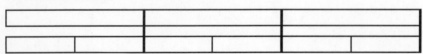

_____ = _____   _____ = _____   _____ = _____

mBook **Reinforce Understanding**
Use the mBook *Study Guide* to review lesson concepts.

Name _____ Date _____

Skills Maintenance
Which One Is Bigger?

Activity 1

Put a check mark next to the larger fraction. Think of a circle to help visualize the fractions.

1. $\frac{2}{3}$ $\frac{1}{4}$

2. $\frac{1}{2}$ $\frac{3}{4}$

3. $\frac{2}{10}$ $\frac{2}{3}$

4. $\frac{1}{8}$ $\frac{6}{8}$

5. $\frac{1}{2}$ $\frac{9}{10}$

Name _____ Date _____

Apply Skills
Fraction Bars and the Number Line

Activity 1

Show the fraction on a fraction bar and number line.

1. $2\frac{3}{4}$
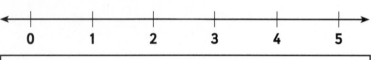

2. $3\frac{1}{3}$
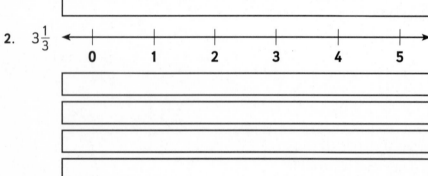

Activity 2

Write the fraction on the number line using the fraction bar.

1.
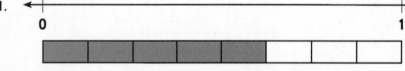

2.
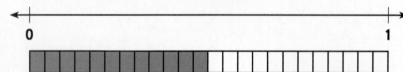

Name _____ Date _____

 ### Problem-Solving Activity
Means, Medians, and Line Plots

Some people earn a lot of money playing golf. Here is how much money the top 14 players made in a golf tournament.

Player	Winnings	Score on Final Day	Total Score for 2002 Tournament
Nick Cash	$1,000,000	72	67–68–70–72–277
John Seymore	$585,000	70	70–73–67–70–280
Cyril Davidson	$252,546	74	68–74–67–74–283
Charles Watkins	$182,882	71	70–76–66–71–285
Mitchell Shepard III	$182,882	69	71–75–70–69–285
Ryan Fine	$182,882	74	69–74–68–74–285
Herman Villalobo	$138,669	75	70–68–73–75–286
Clint Vanwiik	$119,357	67	73–74–73–67–287
Brian Birza	$102,338	76	73–71–68–76–288
Marcos Quenta	$102,338	71	73–73–70–72–288
Kanoa Fujita	$102,338	73	69–76–70–73–288
Antoine Toca	$86,372	73	76–67–73–73–289
Hans Wagner	$68,995	72	76–72–70–72–290
Rusty Pickens	$68,995	71	72–72–75–71–290

Make a line plot of the scores for the last day. Then use a calculator to answer the questions.

1. What was the mean score for the final day? _____

2. What was the range in scores for the final day? _____

3. What was the median score? _____

4. What was the range in salaries? _____

Unit 8

Name _____ Date _____

Skills Maintenance
Fractions on a Number Line

Activity 1

Shade the fraction bars to show each of the fractions. Then tell which part of the fraction is the denominator and which part is the numerator.

1. $\frac{1}{3}$

Denominator _____   Numerator _____

2. $\frac{4}{5}$

Denominator _____   Numerator _____

3. $\frac{5}{8}$

Denominator _____   Numerator _____

Name _____ Date _____

Unit Review
Concept of Fractions

Activity 1

Fill in the missing fractional parts on the number line. Write the decimal number above the line and the fraction below the line.

1.

```
15      15¼              16              16¾   17                          18
```

2.

```
0    ⅓      1          2          3       3⅔  4              5
```

Activity 2

Show the common fractions by drawing different shapes.

1. Show $\frac{1}{3}$ using a circle. ◯

2. Show $\frac{8}{2}$ using triangles. △ △ △ △

3. Show $\frac{3}{5}$ using a circle. ◯

Activity 3

Find equivalent fractions by using the fraction bars.

1. Halves and eighths

_____ = _____   _____ = _____

2. Thirds and sixths

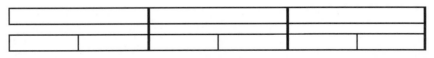

_____ = _____   _____ = _____   _____ = _____

Unit 8

Name _____ Date _____

Unit Review
Analyzing Data

Activity 1

Make two stem-and-leaf plots. The first one should show burger sales on Saturday and the second should show burger sales on Sunday.

Monday's Burger Sales	
10–11 am	19
11 am–12 pm	28
12–1 pm	47
1–2 pm	35
2–3 pm	21
3–4 pm	20
4–5 pm	27
5–6 pm	41
6–7 pm	31
7–8 pm	26
8–9 pm	24

Time	Tue.	Wed.	Thurs.	Fri.	Sat.	Sun.
10–11 am	21	26	20	17	25	16
11 am–12 pm	30	29	33	27	34	31
12–1 pm	48	45	44	49	54	51
1–2 pm	34	31	33	36	39	35
2–3 pm	20	19	23	18	26	22
3–4 pm	19	21	22	18	24	17
4–5 pm	28	31	26	24	32	25
5–6 pm	44	41	45	43	49	42
6–7 pm	33	32	34	30	35	28
7–8 pm	24	27	25	24	30	23
8–9 pm	21	23	22	25	27	20

Burger Sales on Saturday

Stems	Leaves

Burger Sales on Sunday

Stems	Leaves

Name _____ Date _____

Activity 2

Find and record the mean, median, minimum, maximum, range, and any outliers for each of the stem-and-leaf plots you made. Use a calculator and round answers to the nearest whole number.

Statistics for Saturday	
Mean	
Median	
Minimum	
Maximum	
Range	
Outliers	

Statistics for Sunday	
Mean	
Median	
Minimum	
Maximum	
Range	
Outliers	

Activity 3

Analyze the data in the line plot.

1. A family went on vacation. When they returned, they looked at the number of pictures they had taken each day on vacation.

Pictures Taken Each Day

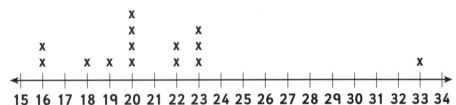

15 16 17 18 19 20 21 22 23 24 25 26 27 28 29 30 31 32 33 34

What is the mean? _____

What is the range? _____

What is the median? _____

What is the outlier? _____

Unit 8

Name _____ Date _____

Skills Maintenance
Fraction Bars

Activity 1

Shade the fraction bars to show the given fraction.

$\frac{3}{5}$

$\frac{5}{6}$

$\frac{7}{10}$

Name _____ Date _____

%÷ Apply Skills
Same Denominator

Activity 1

Circle the problems that can be added or subtracted without changing the denominator.

$\frac{7}{10} + \frac{3}{10}$ $\qquad$ $\frac{2}{3} - \frac{1}{7}$ $\qquad$ $\frac{9}{12} - \frac{4}{12}$

$\frac{4}{5} - \frac{4}{5}$ $\qquad$ $\frac{3}{4} - \frac{1}{5}$ $\qquad$ $\frac{2}{5} - \frac{1}{5}$

$\frac{2}{10} - \frac{10}{2}$ $\qquad$ $\frac{1}{12} - \frac{1}{2}$ $\qquad$ $\frac{7}{8} + \frac{1}{8}$

$\frac{3}{9} - \frac{2}{3}$ $\qquad$ $\frac{3}{4} - \frac{1}{4}$ $\qquad$ $\frac{7}{8} - \frac{7}{16}$

Activity 2

Solve.

1. $\frac{1}{3} + \frac{1}{3}$ _____

2. $\frac{2}{6} + \frac{3}{6}$ _____

3. $\frac{4}{5} + \frac{1}{5}$ _____

4. $\frac{9}{10} - \frac{6}{10}$ _____

5. $\frac{11}{12} - \frac{5}{12}$ _____

6. $\frac{4}{9} - \frac{1}{9}$ _____

Name _____ Date _____

 Problem-Solving Activity
Everyday Measurements

Solve the problems based on the table of liquid measurement.

Table of Liquid Measurement		
16 ounces	1 pint	
32 ounces	2 pints	1 quart
128 ounces	4 quarts	1 gallon
4,032 ounces	$31\frac{1}{2}$ gallons	1 barrel

1. Lunar Imports decided that it wanted to put the 768 ounces of oil into quart containers. How many quarts could it get from the 768 ounces?

   _____

2. There were nine large cans of oil in the shipment. One large can contains 768 ounces of oil. How many total ounces of oil were in the shipment? Is that more or less than one barrel?

   _____

3. One of the stores that buys from Lunar Imports is Jimmy's Food to Go. It is a fast-food restaurant, and it uses one quart of oil a day. If it buys five gallons of oil, how many days will the oil last?

   _____

4. Lunar decided to put the oil from one large can (768 ounces) into pint bottles. How many pint bottles did it get from the large can?

   _____

mBook Reinforce Understanding
Use the mBook *Study Guide* to review lesson concepts.

Name _____ Date _____

Skills Maintenance
Finding Fractions That Have the Same Fair Shares

Activity 1

Circle the problems that you can add or subtract without finding a common denominator. Then solve those problems.

1. $\frac{3}{8} + \frac{2}{8}$

2. $\frac{6}{12} - \frac{5}{10}$

3. $\frac{4}{9} - \frac{2}{9}$

4. $\frac{5}{7} - \frac{2}{9}$

5. $\frac{3}{6} - \frac{2}{6}$

6. $\frac{8}{12} + \frac{1}{12}$

7. $\frac{4}{9} + \frac{3}{9}$

8. $\frac{1}{3} + \frac{1}{3}$

9. $\frac{4}{16} - \frac{2}{11}$

Unit 9

Name _____ Date _____

 Apply Skills
Working With Fractions Greater Than 1

Activity 1

Solve the addition and subtraction problems. Circle the fractions greater than 1.

1. $\frac{3}{4} + \frac{2}{4}$ _____

2. $\frac{5}{9} + \frac{1}{9}$ _____

3. $\frac{8}{12} - \frac{4}{12}$ _____

4. $\frac{10}{9} - \frac{3}{9}$ _____

Activity 2

Solve the word problems.

1. Gena's birthday cake is divided into eight parts. Her brother Tony ate $\frac{2}{8}$ and her sister Carmen ate $\frac{1}{8}$. How much did Tony and Carmen eat?

_____

2. Latisha is trying to build a dog house. She is using boards that are $\frac{3}{4}$ of an inch thick. She tries to use a board that is $\frac{1}{4}$ inch thick but it doesn't work. What is the difference in the thickness of the two boards?

_____

Name _____ Date _____

Problem-Solving Activity
Measuring Time

Answer the questions about time.

1. Lunar Imports uses a fax machine to place orders in other countries. Sometimes it takes a long time to send a fax. Last week, the company sent a fax to South America. The fax took 240 seconds. How many minutes was that?

    _____

2. A ship carrying furniture is coming from Europe. It is going to go all of the way from Denmark to Los Angeles. The captain says that the trip will probably take 35 days. How many weeks is that?

    _____

3. Some of the items that Lunar Imports is going to sell have not been made yet. For example, the company is going to sell little music players that will be made in China. But the people in China have to build the factory first. They think it will take 36 months to build the factory. How many years is that? How many days is that?

    _____

4. When Lunar Imports sells something to a company, Lunar gives the company 90 days to pay for the goods. How many months is that?

    _____

5. Lunar Imports just received a shipment of videos from Canada. The table shows the name of each video and how long it is. Figure out how many hours each video is.

Name of Video	Minutes	Hours
Three Flowers and a Girl	240	
The Spy From Denver	120	
Crime on a Train	300	
Cave of the Bats	180	

mBook **Reinforce Understanding**
Use the mBook *Study Guide* to review lesson concepts.

Unit 9

Name _____ Date _____

 Skills Maintenance
Adding and Subtracting Fractions With the Same Denominator

Activity 1

Add or subtract the fractions.

1. $\frac{1}{4} + \frac{1}{4}$ _____

2. $\frac{3}{6} + \frac{2}{6}$ _____

3. $\frac{11}{12} - \frac{5}{12}$ _____

4. $\frac{4}{8} - \frac{3}{8}$ _____

Activity 2

Add or subtract the fractions. Some of the fractions are greater than 1.
Use fraction bars if necessary.

1. $\frac{3}{6} + \frac{5}{6}$ _____

2. $\frac{1}{5} + \frac{6}{5}$ _____

3. $\frac{7}{4} - \frac{3}{4}$ _____

4. $\frac{14}{12} - \frac{9}{12}$ _____

Name _____ Date _____

Apply Skills
More With Subtraction of Fractions

Activity 1

Shade the fraction bars to represent the subtraction problems.

1. $\dfrac{5}{9} - \dfrac{2}{9}$ _____

2. $\dfrac{2}{3} - \dfrac{1}{3}$ _____

3. $\dfrac{6}{10} - \dfrac{1}{10}$ _____

4. $\dfrac{10}{8} - \dfrac{2}{8}$ _____

5. $\dfrac{4}{4} - \dfrac{4}{4}$ _____

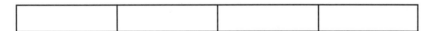

6. $\dfrac{12}{12} - \dfrac{11}{12}$ _____

7. $\dfrac{4}{6} - \dfrac{3}{6}$ _____

8. $\dfrac{4}{7} - \dfrac{2}{7}$ _____

Unit 9

Name _____ Date _____

Problem-Solving Activity
More With Converting Units

Decide the best method for solving the conversion problems with remainders—long division or a calculator. Circle the best method. Then use the conversion chart to do the conversion.

Table of Time Units	
24 hours	1 day
12 months	1 year
365 days	1 year

1. 75 hours = _____

   Circle best method: Long Division   or   Calculator

   Solve the Conversion:

   Units: _____ and _____

2. 30 months = _____

   Circle best method: Long Division   or   Calculator

   Solve the Conversion:

   Units: _____ and _____

3. 2,000 days = _____

   Circle best method: Long Division   or   Calculator

   Solve the Conversion:

   Units: _____ and _____

mBook Reinforce Understanding
Use the mBook *Study Guide* to review lesson concepts.

344   Unit 9 • Lesson 3

Name _____ Date _____

 Skills Maintenance
Finding the Fractions That Have the Same Fair Shares

Activity 1

Circle the problems that can be added or subtracted without finding a common denominator. Then solve them.

1. $\frac{14}{12} - \frac{4}{12}$

2. $\frac{7}{9} + \frac{9}{9}$

3. $1 - \frac{2}{9}$

4. $\frac{3}{4} - \frac{12}{10}$

5. $\frac{4}{8} - \frac{2}{8}$

6. $\frac{4}{6} + \frac{8}{6}$

7. $\frac{4}{3} + \frac{2}{3}$

8. $\frac{1}{2} - \frac{1}{4}$

9. $\frac{3}{7} + \frac{2}{7}$

Name _____ Date _____

Apply Skills
Common Denominators

Activity 1

Use fraction bars to find equivalent fractions with the same denominators. Then solve. Show your fraction bars and work on a separate piece of paper.

1. $\frac{1}{4} + \frac{1}{2} =$ _____

2. $\frac{1}{3} + \frac{1}{2} =$ _____

3. $\frac{2}{3} - \frac{2}{6} =$ _____

Activity 2

Use fraction bars to find equivalent fractions with the same denominators. Then solve. Write the equation and the answer for each problem.

1. Rene ate $\frac{1}{3}$ of a pizza and Adrienne ate $\frac{2}{6}$ of the same pizza. How much of the pizza did the boys eat altogether?

    _____

2. A king gave $\frac{1}{2}$ of his kingdom to his son, Zach. He gave $\frac{1}{3}$ of his kingdom to his daughter, Caroline. Who received the bigger fraction of the kingdom? How much bigger was that person's share?

    _____

    _____

3. Janelle and Sarah made identical cakes. Janelle cut her cake into 6 equal pieces. She ate 1 piece of the cake. Sarah cut her cake into 4 equal pieces, and she ate 1 piece of her cake. Who ate the bigger piece of cake? How much bigger was it?

    _____

    _____

Name _____ Date _____

Problem-Solving Activity
Measuring Dry Weight

Answer the questions.

Table of Dry Weight Units	
16 drams	1 ounce
16 ounces	1 pound
100 pounds	1 hundredweight
2,000 pounds	1 ton

1. Each box of Chilean grapes to be shipped to Lunar Imports weighs 325 ounces. Each box is supposed to weigh less than 25 pounds. How much does each box weigh in pounds and ounces? Do these boxes meet the requirement for weight?

    _____

2. If 450 boxes of figs are delivered to Lunar Imports from Egypt and each of the boxes weighs 10 pounds, how much does the entire shipment weigh in tons and pounds?

    _____

3. The Buzz Coffee Company shipped 250 pounds of coffee beans from Argentina to Lunar Imports. Lunar's workers need to repackage the coffee beans into 8-ounce packages. How many 8-ounce packages can they get from this shipment?

    _____

4. What unit of measure is the same as 100 pounds?

    _____

Unit 9

mBook Reinforce Understanding
Use the mBook *Study Guide* to review lesson concepts.

Name _____ Date _____

Skills Maintenance
Finding Equivalent Fractions

Activity 1

Use the fraction bars to help you fill in the blank in each equivalent fractions equation.

1. $\frac{3}{4} = \frac{}{8}$

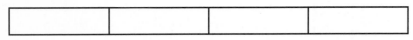

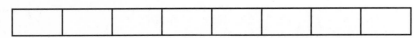

2. $\frac{1}{2} = \frac{}{8}$

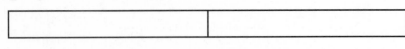

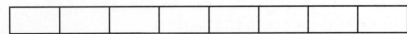

Activity 2

Use fraction bars if necessary to solve the problems. Some of the fractions already have fair shares. Others will have to be changed to equivalent fractions with the same denominator before solving.

1. $\frac{1}{2} + \frac{1}{8}$ _____

2. $\frac{2}{3} - \frac{1}{3}$ _____

3. $\frac{3}{4} - \frac{1}{2}$ _____

Name _____ Date _____

Problem–Solving Activity
Using More Than One Table of Information

Use the tables to help you find the answers. For each problem, tell which category of shipping costs will apply:

(a) Less than 1 pound   (b) Price per pound   (c) Price per ton

Write (a), (b), or (c) on the line.

Table of Dry Weight Units	
16 drams	1 ounce
16 ounces	1 pound
100 pounds	1 hundredweight
2,000 pounds	1 ton

Table of Shipping Costs	
Weight	**Cost**
Less than 1 pound	$5.00
Price per pound	$2.00
Price per ton	$950.00

1. Lunar Imports wants to ship five boxes of frozen meat to a customer in Los Angeles. Each box weighs 480 ounces.

   _____

2. There are 500 crates of oranges in the warehouse in Sydney. Each box weighs 8 pounds.

   _____

3. Lunar Imports received 150 pounds of beef one day and then received 350 pounds of beef the next. A customer wants to have all of this beef shipped to Los Angeles.

   _____

4. The latest shipment of wool from the Sydney Woolen Company came into Lunar Imports yesterday. The shipment contained 100 boxes that weighed 60 pounds each.

   _____

mBook **Reinforce Understanding**
Use the mBook *Study Guide* to review lesson concepts.

Unit 9

Name _____ Date _____

Skills Maintenance
Finding Fractions With the Same Fair Shares

Activity 1

Circle the problems that can be added or subtracted without finding a common denominator. Add or subtract the fractions with like denominators.

1. $\dfrac{4}{12} - \dfrac{4}{12}$

2. $\dfrac{6}{9} + \dfrac{1}{9}$

3. $\dfrac{2}{8} - \dfrac{2}{9}$

4. $\dfrac{3}{4} - \dfrac{2}{10}$

5. $\dfrac{1}{9} - \dfrac{2}{8}$

6. $\dfrac{4}{6} + \dfrac{8}{3}$

7. $\dfrac{8}{3} + \dfrac{2}{3}$

8. $\dfrac{1}{4} - \dfrac{1}{4}$

9. $\dfrac{2}{7} + \dfrac{6}{7}$

Name _____ Date _____

 Apply Skills
Multiplying Fractions by 1

Activity 1

Fill in the blanks in the problems. Make sure the fraction you are
multiplying by is equal to 1.

Model	$\frac{2}{2} = 1$
	$\frac{3}{3} = 1$

1. $\frac{2}{3} \cdot \dfrac{}{} = \dfrac{}{12}$

2. $\frac{3}{4} \cdot \dfrac{}{2} = \dfrac{}{}$

3. $\frac{1}{3} \cdot \dfrac{}{3} = \dfrac{}{}$

4. $\dfrac{}{4} \cdot \frac{5}{5} = \dfrac{15}{}$

5. $\frac{3}{9} \cdot \dfrac{}{2} = \dfrac{}{}$

6. $\frac{1}{2} \cdot \dfrac{}{4} = \dfrac{4}{}$

Unit 9

Name _____ Date _____

Problem-Solving Activity
More Measurement Using Two Tables

Use the tables to answer the questions. You may use a calculator.

Table of Linear Measurement	
12 inches	1 foot
36 inches	1 yard
3 feet	1 yard
5,280 feet	1 mile
1,770 yards	1 mile

Table of Surface Measurement	
144 square inches	1 square foot
9 square feet	1 square yard
640 acres	1 square mile

1. The runway for the new Lunar Imports Center is 2,500 yards long.
    How many miles and yards is that?

    _____

2. The hangar is 202,500 square feet. How many square yards is that?

    _____

3. The longest factory at Lunar Imports Center is 590 yards long.
    How many feet is that?

    _____

4. The height of the warehouse has to be big enough to park a cargo
    plane inside. The biggest plane is 44 feet high. The height of the
    factory door is 16 yards. Is the door tall enough for the plane to
    get through?

    _____

5. Lunar Imports Center is built on 4,480 acres of land outside of
    Nashville. How many square miles is that?

    _____

mBook Reinforce Understanding
Use the mBook *Study Guide* to review lesson concepts.

Name _____ Date _____

Skills Maintenance
Working With Fractions

Activity 1

Solve the problems.

1. $\frac{2}{3} \cdot \frac{3}{3}$ _____

2. $\frac{4}{5} \cdot \frac{2}{2}$ _____

3. $\frac{3}{4} \cdot \frac{4}{4}$ _____

Activity 2

Fill in the blanks. Make sure the fraction you are multiplying by is equal to 1.

Model	$\frac{2}{2} = 1, \frac{3}{3} = 1$

1. $\frac{2}{4} \cdot \frac{\ \ }{\ \ } = \frac{\ \ }{8}$

2. $\frac{3}{5} \cdot \frac{\ \ }{4} = \frac{\ \ }{\ \ }$

3. $\frac{2}{3} \cdot \frac{\ \ }{\ \ } = \frac{10}{\ \ }$

4. $\frac{5}{7} \cdot \frac{\ \ }{3} = \frac{\ \ }{\ \ }$

5. $\frac{1}{6} \cdot \frac{\ \ }{\ \ } = \frac{2}{\ \ }$

Activity 3

Solve.

1. $\frac{3}{5} + \frac{2}{10}$ _____

2. $\frac{4}{7} + \frac{1}{3} =$ _____

3. $\frac{7}{10} + \frac{8}{20}$ _____

4. $\frac{13}{15} - \frac{2}{5}$ _____

5. $\frac{3}{4} - \frac{1}{16}$ _____

6. $\frac{8}{11} - \frac{15}{22}$ _____

Unit 9

Name _____ Date _____

%÷ Apply Skills
Fractions on a Ruler

Activity 1

Use a ruler to measure the lines to the closest $\frac{1}{4}$, $\frac{1}{2}$, $\frac{3}{4}$, or whole inch.
Circle the correct answer.

1. _____

    How long? $\frac{1}{4}$ in. $\frac{1}{2}$ in. $\frac{3}{4}$ in.   1 in. $1\frac{1}{2}$ in.   2 in.

2. _____

    How long? $\frac{1}{4}$ in. $\frac{1}{2}$ in. $\frac{3}{4}$ in.   1 in. $1\frac{1}{2}$ in.   2 in.

3. _____

    How long? $\frac{1}{4}$ in. $\frac{1}{2}$ in. $\frac{3}{4}$ in.   1 in. $1\frac{1}{2}$ in.   2 in.

4. __

    How long? $\frac{1}{4}$ in. $\frac{1}{2}$ in. $\frac{3}{4}$ in.   1 in. $1\frac{1}{2}$ in.   2 in.

Name _____ Date _____

 Problem-Solving Activity
Measuring Objects

Use pencil, paper, a ruler, a calculator, and the table to answer the questions about each car.

Table of Linear Measurement	
12 inches	1 foot
36 inches	1 yard
3 feet	1 yard

1. How long is this car from front to back? _____

2. The box it will be packaged in is four inches long. How many feet of shelf space will the cars take if you put six boxes on a shelf as in the drawing below? _____

| sports car | sports car | sports car | sports car | sports car | sports car |

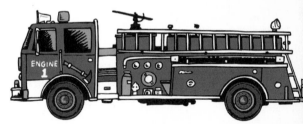

Racing Car   **Fire Truck**

3. How long is the racing car from the front to the back? _____

4. How long is the fire truck from front to back? _____

5. About how much longer is the racing car than the fire truck? _____

mBook Reinforce Understanding
Use the mBook *Study Guide* to review lesson concepts.

Name _____ Date _____

 Skills Maintenance
Multiplying Fractions

Activity 1

Solve the problems.

1. $\frac{3}{4} \cdot \frac{2}{2}$ _____

2. $\frac{5}{6} \cdot \frac{3}{3}$ _____

3. $\frac{1}{4} \cdot \frac{4}{4}$ _____

4. $\frac{5}{6} \cdot \frac{3}{5}$ _____

5. $\frac{8}{9} \cdot \frac{2}{2}$ _____

6. $\frac{3}{7} \cdot \frac{5}{5}$ _____

Name _____ Date _____

 Apply Skills
Finding Common Denominators for Two Fractions

Activity 1

Find the least common denominator for each pair of numbers. Then multiply the fractions in each problem by a fraction equal to 1 to give you equivalent fractions with the least common denominator. Finally, rewrite the problem and solve it.

1. $\frac{1}{2} - \frac{1}{3}$ What is the least common denominator? _____

   $\frac{1}{2} \cdot$ _____ = _____ $\frac{1}{3} \cdot$ _____ = _____

   Rewrite the problem and solution here:

2. $\frac{1}{4} + \frac{1}{3}$ What is the least common denominator? _____

   $\frac{1}{4} \cdot$ _____ = _____ $\frac{1}{3} \cdot$ _____ = _____

   Rewrite the problem and solution here:

3. $\frac{1}{3} - \frac{1}{5}$ What is the least common denominator? _____

   $\frac{1}{3} \cdot$ _____ = _____ $\frac{1}{5} \cdot$ _____ = _____

   Rewrite the problem and solution here:

4. $\frac{2}{3} + \frac{1}{4}$ What is the least common denominator? _____

   $\frac{2}{3} \cdot$ _____ = _____ $\frac{1}{4} \cdot$ _____ = _____

   Rewrite the problem and solution here:

Unit 9

Name _____ Date _____

Problem-Solving Activity
Fractions in the Real World

Solve the problems by finding a common denominator.

1. Deedra ran $\frac{1}{5}$ of a mile before softball practice and $\frac{1}{2}$ of a mile after practice. How far did she run before and after practice?

    _____

2. Deedra plays third base for her team. She spends $\frac{1}{4}$ of the practice catching ground balls. Rene, who plays left field, spends $\frac{3}{8}$ of her time catching fly balls. What is the difference between the time Deedra and Rene spend practicing catching?

    _____

3. Deedra's team plays $\frac{1}{4}$ of its games out of town and $\frac{1}{3}$ of its games at other high schools in her town. What fraction of its games does Deedra's team play away from Deedra's school?

    _____

mBook **Reinforce Understanding**
Use the mBook *Study Guide* to review lesson concepts.

Name _____ Date _____

Skills Maintenance
Add and Subtract Fractions

Activity 1

Solve.

1. $\frac{3}{4} + \frac{4}{5}$ _____

2. $\frac{1}{2} + \frac{3}{4}$ _____

3. $\frac{4}{8} + \frac{1}{4}$ _____

4. $\frac{11}{12} - \frac{2}{4}$ _____

5. $\frac{2}{3} - \frac{1}{2}$ _____

6. $\frac{5}{9} - \frac{1}{3}$ _____

Unit 9

Name _____ Date _____

Problem-Solving Activity
Write a Word Problem Using Common Conversions

Write four fraction word problems using units of measurement that were
discussed in this unit. Include at least two fractions in each problem.
These fractions should have different denominators. Provide the answer
to each problem. Write your problems on a separate piece of paper.

Table of Dry Weight Units	
16 drams	1 ounce
16 ounces	1 pound
100 pounds	1 hundredweight
2,000 pounds	1 ton

Table of Time Units	
60 seconds	1 minute
60 minutes	1 hour
24 hours	1 day
7 days	1 week
30 days*	1 month
12 months	1 year
365 days	1 year
100 years	1 century

Table of Liquid Measurement		
1 pint		16 ounces
1 quart	2 pints	32 ounces
1 gallon	4 quarts	128 ounces
1 barrel	$31\frac{1}{2}$ gallons	4,032 ounces

Table of Linear Measurement	
12 inches	1 foot
36 inches	1 yard
3 feet	1 yard
5,280 feet	1 mile
1,770 yards	1 mile

Table of Surface Measurement	
144 square inches	1 square foot
9 square feet	1 square yard
640 square acres	1 square mile

mBook Reinforce Understanding
Use the mBook *Study Guide* to review lesson concepts.

Name _____ Date _____

 ## Skills Maintenance
Add and Subtract Fractions

Activity 1

Circle the problems that can be added or subtracted without having to find a common denominator.

$\frac{7}{9} + \frac{3}{9}$ $\frac{3}{4} - \frac{1}{4}$ $\frac{7}{8} + \frac{1}{5}$

$\frac{2}{3} - \frac{1}{2}$ $\frac{5}{5} - \frac{1}{5}$ $\frac{3}{9} - \frac{2}{9}$

Activity 2

Solve.

1. $\frac{2}{4} \cdot \frac{3}{3} =$ _____

2. $\frac{1}{6} \cdot \frac{4}{4} =$ _____

3. $\frac{3}{8} \cdot \frac{2}{2} =$ _____

4. $\frac{7}{8} \cdot \frac{2}{2} =$ _____

5. $\frac{5}{9} \cdot \frac{3}{3} =$ _____

6. $\frac{1}{3} \cdot \frac{5}{5} =$ _____

Unit 9

Name _____ Date _____

 Unit Review
Adding and Subtracting Fractions

Activity 1

Use fraction bars to find a common denominator for each set of fractions.

1. $\frac{1}{5}$ and $\frac{2}{3}$ Common denominator _____

2. $\frac{3}{4}$ and $\frac{1}{6}$ Common denominator _____

Activity 2

Add or subtract the fractions. First, you will have to find a common denominator. Use each of the following strategies at least once:

- tables of multiples

- fact families

- number lines

1. $\frac{2}{3} + \frac{4}{5} =$ _____

2. $\frac{1}{4} + \frac{3}{3} =$ _____

3. $\frac{2}{7} + \frac{3}{5} =$ _____

4. $\frac{2}{2} - \frac{4}{4} =$ _____

5. $\frac{1}{2} - \frac{1}{3} =$ _____

Name _____ Date _____

Unit Review
Working With Data

Activity 1

Convert. Then check your answer with a calculator.

1.   26 inches = _____ feet and _____ inches

2.   5 yards = _____ feet

3.   8,950 yards = _____ miles and _____ yards

4.   6 acres = _____ square yards

5.   288 ounces = _____ quarts

6.   30 quarts = _____ gallons and _____ quarts

7.   400 years = _____ centuries

8.   7 weeks = _____ days

9.   200 minutes = _____ hours and _____ minutes

10. 36 drams = _____ ounces and _____ drams

Activity 2

Use one of the problems in Activity 1 to write your own word problem.

_____

_____

_____

_____

mBook Reinforce Understanding
Use the mBook *Study Guide* to review lesson concepts.